THE
CAUSE
WITHIN YOU

FOUNDER OF THE DREAM CENTER

MATTHEW BARNETT

WITH GEORGE BARNA

THE
CAUSE
WITHIN YOU

FINDING THE ONE GREAT THING YOU WERE
CREATED TO DO IN THIS WORLD

BARNA
AN IMPRINT OF
TYNDALE HOUSE PUBLISHERS, INC.

Visit Tyndale's Web site at www.tyndale.com.

TYNDALE is a registered trademark of Tyndale House Publishers, Inc.

Barna and the Barna logo are trademarks of George Barna.

BarnaBooks is an imprint of Tyndale House Publishers, Inc.

The Cause within You: Finding the One Great Thing You Were Created to Do in This World

Copyright © 2011 by Matthew Barnett. All rights reserved.

Cover photos by Stephen Vosloo, copyright © by Tyndale House Publishers, Inc. All rights reserved.

Designed by Beth Sparkman

Published in association with Esther Fedorkevich and the literary agency of Fedd and Company, Inc., 606 Flamingo Blvd., Austin, TX 78734.

Library of Congress Cataloging-in-Publication Data

Barnett, Matthew.
  The cause within you : finding the one great thing you were created to do in this world / Matthew Barnett with George Barna.
    p. cm.
  Includes bibliographical references.
  ISBN 978-1-4143-4846-9 (hc)
  1. Dreams—Religious aspects—Christianity. 2. God (Christianity)—Will. 3. Barnett, Matthew.
4. Los Angeles International Church (Los Angeles, Calif.) I. Barna, George. II. Title.
  BR115.D74B36 2011
  259.086'9420979494—dc22   201004624

Printed in the United States of America

17 16 15 14 13 12 11
 7   6   5   4

*I would like to dedicate this book to my
Lord and Savior Jesus Christ, who inspired this cause;
my gorgeous wife, Caroline; my "angel" Mia;
my "little buddy" Caden; the Barnett family;
and the greatest generation of cause-driven volunteers
at the Dream Center. They are changing the world!*

Contents

Foreword

THERE ARE THREE THINGS you need to know about my son Matthew.

The first thing is that every day, every opportunity, every new person he meets gets him charged up. I've never seen anyone love life more; he can't wait to get up in the morning. Because of that, people like to be around him. He's like the Pied Piper—just full of fun, everywhere he goes—and he's always building people up through his positive attitude.

The second thing is that he can keep more balls in the air at one time, and do it well, than anybody I've ever met. Just take a look at the Dream Center, an inner-city ministry offering an amazing number and variety of programs. Against all odds, a twenty-year-old boy got things started because he allowed God to work through him. Today, because he perseveres with that same spirit, Matthew keeps all the programs going—and going strong.

The third is that he has a generous spirit. Matthew is the most giving person I know. Not only is he free with his time and encouragement, on a practical level he can't carry much cash on him because by the time he gets to wherever he's going, he's given it all away to people in need!

Now let me ask you . . . does this sound like the kind of life you want to be living? Does the idea of all this passion and purpose excite you? Do you want people to talk about you this way? It is more than possible; it is God's dream for you.

The reason Matthew lives this way is because he is driven by the special cause God has planted within him: when he sees somebody with a need, he feels called to fill it. That's how he's built the Dream Center ministry, which you'll read about in this book. At the Dream Center, we follow Jesus' example of finding a need and meeting it; finding a hurt and healing it. Jesus built his own church up on healing and helping and reaching out to people. So when Matthew sees a hurt, he doesn't get discouraged; he views it as a great opportunity to do something for God.

If I can tell you one thing for sure, it is this: everybody must have a cause if they're going to be happy in life. You need something that makes you want to wake up in the morning, excited, ready to face the day. Matthew is that way because he's discovered his cause, and that's what makes his life. If you're living for something that's *not* your cause, you may reach your dream, but it's going to feel disappointing, like a letdown. Your fun is in climbing, in pursuing your cause. And the reason the cause makes your life is that you never run out of it. You will *always* have something to give. So if happiness to you is palms up—living only for what you receive—you'll only be happy at your birthday and Christmas. But if you have a cause, happiness is your palms down—what you can give to other people—because the need will always be there.

Matthew discovered his calling at a young age. Let me tell you, though, if you are feeling the drive to discover your cause, what I want to say to you is that *it's never too late*. I see it all the time in my church—you're going along with life and then you get a little tap on the shoulder, a prompting, telling you that maybe God is directing you another way. Maybe you're successful in your line of work, maybe you have a good income, and you're pretty well set for life, but you find it doesn't scratch the itch in your heart. I guarantee that you may have more to bring to your cause than even someone who knows theirs at a young age. I see older people who begin to act on their cause later in life, and in many cases they have far more qualifications than someone like me who went directly into ministry. They've got passion, drive, business ability, and—most importantly—the freshness that comes with making a new beginning.

Let me tell you a story about Matthew and me that shows how perfectly God's plan works, how he ordains us to be exactly where he wants us, right in his will, living out our causes.

When the leaders of my denomination first approached me about pioneering a ministry in Los Angeles, they said there was nothing there yet but a dream. They were hoping I could shepherd Bethel Temple, a small, historic church in the denomination, back to health. When they asked me to pray about the opportunity, I couldn't exactly say no! And secretly, my heart leaped within me. I hadn't told them this, but when I was twenty years old and on my way to Bethel Temple to hold a revival, I drove past the Angelus Temple. I had a strong feeling—I believe it was a prompting of the Holy Spirit—that one day I would pastor a church in this area. I had hidden that feeling in my heart all those years.

When I decided to accept the opportunity, I knew I needed somebody to work with. I began talking to potential candidates—they'd get very excited on the phone, but when they'd go to LA and see the run-down area where they'd be ministering, suddenly they'd change their minds.

Now, one of my more well-known sermons at the time was called "The Miracle in the House." It's based on the idea that everything you need to build a great church is in your house. And one day, a man in my church who knew I'd been searching for a ministry partner said, "Pastor, you're foolish! You're searching and searching for the right person to help you when the miracle is right in your house!"

"Matthew is just a twenty-year-old boy," I retorted.

"Yeah, but I've heard you preach, 'Don't despise a person's youth.'"

I just hate it when they use my own preaching against me.

After several others came to me with the same counsel, and after much thought, I asked Matthew to join me in LA as co-pastor. He accepted, and Bethel Temple later merged with Angelus Temple. But what Matthew didn't tell me—what I didn't learn until years later—was this:

"When I was sixteen," he ultimately told me, "I was standing outside, looking up at the stars one Sunday night after church. As I was praying, the Lord impressed upon my heart that by the age of twenty I'd be pastoring a church in LA."

I looked at him, shocked. I had no idea he had wanted to go to LA, and at that age he didn't know about my calling to the Angelus Temple. "I didn't want to tell you that at first, Dad, in case it might influence your decision to ask me to go. I knew that God would have to be the one to tell you, not me."

And He did. And you're about to learn what happened as a result.

More important, you're going to learn how to discover the cause God has for you, just as God steered Matthew to the people in inner-city Los Angeles who needed hope and healing. This is how we build a life: find people with needs and try to fill them, and you'll see how happy it makes you. Live vicariously through them. It's the highest form of living, because you give up a little of something you want so that other people can have a lot of it. That's really what Matthew has done. He's given up a lot of his life so that a lot of people can turn their lives around.

Read this book and discover what *your* cause is. Trust me: finding it will make your life.

Pastor Tommy Barnett
First Assembly of God in Phoenix

CHAPTER I

A NIGHT ON THE STREETS

SOMETHING STIRRED ME AWAKE. I struggled to open my eyes. My surroundings slowly came into focus. It was dark, with rays of light off to the side that barely penetrated my peripheral vision. I heard indistinct noises nearby, a kind of low mumbling coming from a few feet away. And I felt a presence. As things came into focus, I found that somebody was staring into my eyes. I stared back and realized it wasn't a some*body*—it was a some*thing*.

I squinted to crystallize the image and realized it was a cat. No, wait, it was a . . . rat. A rat the size of a cat! Supersized. Its eyes were maybe three inches from mine, its whiskers even closer. Other than the twitching of its nostrils as it catalogued my scent, it was perfectly still, studying me with obvious hostility.

Now I was awake, aware of where I was and what was happening. I remembered having carefully placed my large sheet of cardboard on the pavement in this alleyway, maybe twenty minutes ago, hoping for an hour of peaceful slumber on the streets of Los Angeles. What was it—four, maybe five o'clock in the morning? An unrhythmic series of moans filled the air from other homeless people lying farther up the alley, doing their best to get some shut-eye. I'd dozed off for a few minutes before this bucktoothed rodent invaded my twelve square feet of prime real estate.

I struggled to my feet, picked up my cardboard bed, and slowly shuffled out of the alley onto the main street. My watch said it was 2:13 a.m. Time was obviously on a holiday tonight. The light from the streetlamps was the only illumination in this part of the city.

I passed by a boarded-up shop and caught the strong, ever-present whiff of urine. That seemed to be the odor of the homeless nation: there were no bathrooms available to us in the dead of night—or during a large share of the day, for that matter. When you had to go, you found a wall in a vacant section of an alley and did your business. The Porta Potties strategically distributed around this section of the city, meant for the homeless, were of no use to us since they'd been hijacked by the prostitutes and drug dealers, who complete their transactions inside those mobile offices. They were the only businesses open 24-7 down here, peddling flesh and pharms. No homeless person in his right mind would enter those disease-riddled fiberglass boxes unless they were completing a deal.

Fellow vagabonds shuffled past me, traveling in the opposite direction. A woman wearing a tattered army jacket and a wraparound skirt that was frayed at her calloused, bare feet hobbled by. Her hair was a mess of tangles, her eyes sunken, wrinkles creasing her forehead as she shuffled along. A frail man who looked to be in his mid-fifties but was probably thirtyish was a few paces behind her, toting a ragged backpack that I suspected contained all of his worldly possessions. Another haggard-looking fellow was ten feet farther down the sidewalk, slumped over one of the parking meters, staring vacantly across the street. He had nowhere to go, no time by which he had to be there. He was simply taking a break from his nightly march to wherever.

These fellow denizens of the streets were dead on their feet, but experience had taught them to keep moving, to stay alert. Darkness was the scourge of life; inactivity was an invitation to danger. While I trooped up and down the streets of skid row, I occasionally looked these passersby straight in the face, searching for signs of hope, but had learned to lower my standards and seek a simple expression of life. Very few returned my gaze. These people were on autopilot, traipsing lifelessly forward, silently repeating the mantra the homeless chant to themselves each night: *Gotta make it 'til sunrise. Gotta make it 'til sunrise. . . .*

As a bloodcurdling scream radiated from around the corner ahead, I ducked into the hollowed-out doorway of a storefront and leaned against the mesh security door for support. I felt an indescribable mixture of emotions: yes, there was fear, but it was tempered by joy, intrigue, excitement, and compassion. You see, I was on skid row *by choice*. This was a one-night-only command performance among the people whom I have spent my entire adult life serving.

I am the pastor of a "megachurch," a proud bastion of Christianity in the heart of downtown Los Angeles. Tonight was the fifteenth anniversary of the beginning of our ministry, known as the Dream Center, in which we help to restore the shattered dreams and empty lives of broken people. To the horror of my church colleagues, and against the advice of many, I decided this was where I wanted to spend that anniversary: living among the very people I have come to love during these past fifteen years.

I was on skid row *by choice*. This was a one-night-only command performance among the people whom I have spent my entire adult life serving.

If I had stayed with the original game plan, I would have been home in my comfortable bed, lying next to my beautiful, loving wife, Caroline, resting peacefully in our single-family house while our two children slept securely down the hall. I would have been dreaming about the incredible celebration that would have taken place earlier in the evening at the special dinner planned for the hundred or so key people who made the Dream Center tick. We would have watched videos of past ministry victories; joyfully sung praises to God; eaten a delicious, well-prepared meal; and listened to people's recollections of how God had done miracle after miracle in our midst and inspired us to keep battling the odds for fifteen years. It would have been a night to remember.

Now, barely five hours into my "alternative celebration," I knew this was certainly a night I would never forget.

A few weeks before, as the planned celebration got closer and the preparations intensified, I felt uneasy in my gut. That's often how God grabs my attention. In response, I spent time praying for Him to clarify what He wanted. Soon it became clear to me that a party to celebrate ourselves was not what God had in mind. I could sense that He was looking for me to do something radical, not something comfortable and self-serving. Unsure what that might be, I enlisted several people from my team to join me in prayer and to wait for further divine direction.

Finally, the solution came into focus: I should spend the anniversary night on the streets of skid row in Los Angeles. I've worked hand in hand with poor and suffering people for fifteen years. I've spent countless hours on the city streets offering to help them and even to transport them from skid row to our campus, where we partnered with them in breaking the bondage of poverty and bad choices. But in those fifteen years I had never spent a night sleeping in their midst, on the concrete. Truthfully, it had never even occurred to me to do so. Wasn't I doing enough already?

Maybe not. The clear impression I received was that God was intent upon pushing me beyond my comfort zone, orchestrating something that would forever change me. Again.

The sheer magnitude of the idea marked it as God's; the absurdity of the option underscored its necessity.

It became obvious that throwing ourselves a party was appropriate by the world's standards, but not by God's. An anniversary gala would be a sign of naive hubris. From the day this ministry began, it was built upon going against the grain, doing the unexpected. A party? The greatest celebration would be to demonstrate solidarity with those I serve, to dig more deeply into their world so I could serve them more profoundly.

So after we had our regular Thursday night service at the church, I put on the clothes I'd grabbed specially for this night—a grimy T-shirt; a generic gray hoodie; a pair of baggy, ill-fitting cargo pants; and sneakers.

My prep team at the church included a tall, slender African American man named Lawrence,* who was one of our security guards. Lawrence originally came to the Dream Center from the same streets to which we were headed. He'd been desperately in need of help, had successfully completed one of our recovery programs, and now had his life on an even keel. When he heard what we were up to, he rushed to my side and begged me not to go. Seeing my resolve, he changed his tactic and insisted on preparing me for the odyssey that lay ahead.

"You don't know what you doing, Pastor," he said respectfully. "Let me get you ready so you can survive the night. There's things you don't know about the streets, and those streets is mean, Pastor. I can teach

---

* In several places in this book the names of individuals have been changed to protect their privacy. The stories are true; only their names have been changed.

you a few things that will help." In retrospect, I believe Lawrence's survival tips may have saved my life.

After we smeared some grease on my face and ruffled my hair, I boarded a church van and was driven to the central business district of Los Angeles. Amidst the towering buildings in center city I disembarked and said a quick prayer with the team members in the van. Then I pulled my large piece of cardboard from the back and trudged the six blocks from the corporate haven to the edge of skid row. I had no money in my pockets; I really wanted to know what it felt like to be homeless. My only protection, at Lawrence's insistence, was a well-worn Bible.

As I strode toward my destination, I again pondered what I was about to do. Was this insane? I wondered. I'm the husband of a wife who loves me, the father of two young children who depend on me, the pastor of a thriving church that gets its direction from me. I'm not indispensable, but was this urban adventure demonstrating the wisdom of a godly man? Did this decision display the discernment of a true leader? Was I engaging in an act of courage, or was it mere foolishness? Was I demeaning the homeless by dressing up and pretending to be one of them? What was the likelihood of even surviving the night?

As a "successful" pastor, was I settling for what was now a routine process that insulated me from the suffering and tragedies that had sparked my ministry so many years ago?

My self-doubts were interrupted by the sight of a genuine homeless guy—not a fake like me— moving toward skid row some twenty feet ahead of me on the otherwise deserted sidewalk. I called out to him and explained who I really was and asked him if he thought I would survive the night. His reply came without emotion or hesitation.

"Nope," he said evenly, looking me in the eye. "You're too clean. They'll sniff you out in a heartbeat. Won't work. Go home." He nodded a silent good-bye and resumed his slow hobble toward the edge of helplessness.

For a moment that seemed like all the convincing I needed. Maybe God had sent him to meet me there, an angel of mercy, to deliver one final warning, a word of sanity to break the spell of lunacy that was propelling me toward disaster. Maybe it was time to call off this whole charade. Who was I trying to fool?

But as I stood there trying to get a firm fix on my emotions, my confidence returned. I wasn't here to perform a circus trick or to get the public's attention—"Hey everyone! Come see the pastor who lived for a night on skid row! Hear tales of bravery and stories of the dark side!" No, I was on the streets because I have come to truly love the unlovable. I have discovered how God can love the people that nobody else wants. And frankly, after fifteen years, I was worried that I'd lost my edge.

As a "successful" pastor, was I settling for what was now a routine process that insulated me from the suffering and tragedies that had sparked my ministry so many years ago? Had I become too comfortable in what we did to serve poor and hurting people? Was I now simply a motivational speaker, a fund-raiser, an organizational figurehead, a ministry expert doing good works but living a safe, sanitized existence?

I turned to watch the homeless man shuffle away from me. In that moment it was clear that God wanted me to do something radical; He wanted me to do *this*. I couldn't imagine anything more radical than humbling myself in this fashion, embracing the same risks that Jesus Christ had adopted when He lived and ministered among the untouchables of His day.

Hanging out on skid row for a day or two, with an open mind and heart, was not meant to be a quaint or clever adventure that would "preach well." It was a necessary recalibration to get me back on track— in sync with the cause God had instilled in me fifteen years before.

CHAPTER 2

LOST AND FOUND IN LA

I GREW UP in a preacher's home. Both my father and grandfather were well-known, successful pastors. Ever since I was sixteen, I have known that God was calling me to be a pastor too.

That may help explain my naive but genuine enthusiasm when, in September 1994, I headed to Los Angeles with my dad, Tommy Barnett, who had been asked to help turn around a struggling congregation in a desperate part of downtown Los Angeles. Dad was already pastoring a very large, well-known, and influential church—First Assembly of God in Phoenix. The leaders of his denomination were hoping that while he continued to pastor the church in Phoenix, he could also provide the kind of leadership that would restore spiritual health to the failing church in LA. He accepted the assignment and decided this would be a good opportunity to give me greater experience in church leadership.

The plan was for my dad and me to be co-pastors. He would fly in from Phoenix on Thursday mornings and stay with me until late Saturday, just in time to catch the last flight back to Phoenix for his Sunday morning services. Meanwhile, I'd be stationed at Bethel Temple full-time, learning under my dad's expert, seasoned guidance.

I was twenty years old at the time. I had never been to Los Angeles, but I was brimming with confidence as I loaded my stuff in our car and drove to LA with my dad, eager to embrace the chance to bring spiritual health to that declining church. And not just any church—it was Bethel Temple, one of the first churches birthed out of the historic Azusa Street Revival. The denomination was determined that such a historic church should not die—and I was just as determined that if it did, it wouldn't be on my watch.

What I did not fully comprehend when we left Phoenix was the current state of that church. Bethel Temple was located in a hard-to-find, dangerous neighborhood. It was an ethnic area; I quickly discovered that I was the only white guy in the vicinity. The church needed a new pastor because the current one was retiring; he was eighty years old. That meant the church would transition from having the oldest active pastor in the denomination to the youngest! The congregation, once vibrant, had dwindled down to just thirty-nine members, of whom the average age was close to that of their exiting pastor. Oh, and did I mention that most of them spoke only Filipino? I didn't even know what Filipino was.

Despite the paltry size of the church, I was excited. Imagine being only twenty years old and having a church to pastor in the second-largest city in the country! I was absolutely determined to build God a great church. In fact, that became my life's mission: *to build God a great church.*

Well, things didn't go exactly as I had expected. I preached my heart out, but in no time at all I had grown the church from thirty-nine people to zero. I don't mean twelve people or five, I mean there was actually a service when not one person showed up! You know the old question, if a tree falls in the forest and nobody is there to hear it, did it make any noise? Well, I can tell you the noise that's made in a church when no one shows up for the services: it's the weeping of its discouraged pastor.

From the day I arrived, my time was consumed by doing all the things I believed a godly, successful pastor would do. My life had been spent preparing for this opportunity. I'd read church-growth books. I had attended numerous conferences where I'd listened with rapt attention to pastors of large churches talk about their strategies. My bedroom wall at home was plastered with poster after poster of motivational quotes and inspirational photos. I didn't see Bethel Temple as a dying church; I saw it as a church in the early stages of being restored to greatness.

I preached my heart out, but in no time at all I had grown the church from thirty-nine people to zero.

So when the church continued to die a slow and painful death, I just couldn't understand what God was doing. I was pretty sure I knew what He *wasn't* doing: He wasn't answering my prayers. He wasn't bringing people to the church. He wasn't restoring a historic church to greatness. He wasn't helping me build a great church. And He sure wasn't concerned about my desire to be a successful pastor.

So one Sunday about three months into my tenure, after yet another disastrous church service, I returned to my tiny apartment, collapsed on the bed, and let loose, saturating my pillow with tears of frustration and muffled cries of anguish and despair. I felt like an utter failure, a total fool. And of course, when you fail in service to God, the guilt is as deep as the ocean: I hadn't just failed, I had failed *God*! In my solitary mourning, I kept asking God why this was happening and what He wanted from me.

No response.

My emptiness knew no bounds. I felt I was being faithful to Him; wasn't He supposed to be faithful to me? What did He want?

11

Finally, He was ready to tell me. While tossing and turning that night, failing to get any real rest, I sensed His presence. It was very late at night, sometime after midnight, but I felt led to walk a few blocks to Echo Park. That's the center of our section of downtown Los Angeles. Trust me, there had to have been a sure sense of God's leading because no young white kid would feel safe in Echo Park in broad daylight, much less in the dead of night. But I dutifully trudged down there, still praying silently for God to bring clarity to my confusion.

I got to the park. What was once a beautiful oasis of lush greenery surrounding graceful swans peacefully paddling around a clear pond with a sparkling fountain in the center was now a mossy body of stagnant water with floating litter and derelicts passed out around its perimeter. The noise and activity in the area shocked me too. After all, it was well past midnight on a Sunday night, yet the place was abuzz.

Of course, the activity was not what you might expect. It was like one giant urban crime scene. It was what I imagined a movie set would be like if a studio were there filming a movie depicting a police force's worst nightmare. To my left were three police cars with twirling red lights ablaze. Behind the vehicles, five armed police officers surrounded two young men sporting handcuffs and leaning spread-eagle against the wall of an apartment building. To my right were a bunch of drunks sitting on the sidewalk and on the front steps of a couple of buildings, with brown paper bags in their hands or at their feet, the ever-present accessory of the alcoholic crowd. Two wobbling drunks were dissing each other in slurred tones, getting ready to square off—or maybe pass out, whichever happened first. There was a helicopter overhead with its powerful searchlight trained on a spot in a nearby neighborhood, presumably assisting street officers in locating an escaping criminal. There were homeless people with shopping carts, drug deals going down in the shadows, and pregnant teenagers looking frightened and very alone.

Honestly, it was like a cartoon—an exaggeration of every ill you try to avoid in the big city, all clustered into a single area adjacent to the park. If I hadn't been so haggard over my own desperate situation, I would have laughed at the magnitude of the calamity—and then run for my life!

Instead, I stood there, taking it all in. *So this is where You brought me, Lord, from the secure suburbs of my upbringing in the desert to the squalor and hopelessness of Los Angeles.* Not the Beverly Hills or Malibu portions of Los Angeles, mind you, but this, ground zero of human depravity. *It's bad enough that You give me a dying church, but a dying neighborhood, too?*

I stared at the scene and silently yelled out to Him one more time.

Look at this mess, Lord! You brought me here. I came willingly, full of hope and excitement and passion. I came here to build You a great church.

At that moment I heard God speak to me—not an audible voice, but the clearest of impressions, an unmistakable reply: *I did not bring you here to build a great church. I brought you here to build people— these people. You build the people. I'll build the church.*

Slap down by God! And He wasn't done.

I don't ever want you to talk or even think about "success" again. Think about being a blessing. Success is obedience to your calling; I have called you to bless these people. Love them. Heal them. Help them. Serve them.

There was a pause as I absorbed that thought. Then came His closing argument.

I love these people. If you reach the people that nobody wants, I'll send you the people that everybody wants.

Stunned, I sat down on a stoop a couple of feet away. *Build people.* It was as if we'd been in a boxing ring and my opponent had slugged me really hard and repeatedly in the stomach. *Serve them.* I wanted to hear from God, and I did. As is often the case, it was not what I expected or perhaps even wanted to hear. *Reach the people that nobody wants.* But it was exactly what I needed to hear. *Bless these people.*

Now I watched all the things taking place around me with new eyes. As understanding settled in, I could feel the excitement of a great cause beginning to build within me. It no longer mattered that I was only twenty or that I was a white guy in **I wanted to hear from** a nonwhite neighborhood. That nobody turned **God, and I did. As is** up at my church service or that the denomina- **often the case, it was** tion probably had something different in mind **not what I expected** seemed less important now. What mattered was **or wanted to hear.** that I'd heard from God, and I knew that if I was willing to bless these outcasts and social losers, something great was going to happen. It was inevitable. After all, God was on my side.

This was my congregation. They just didn't know it yet.

Somehow my worst nightmare had turned into my greatest thrill. After a well-intentioned false start, I was finally en route to fulfilling my cause. God was in it. Clearly, this was going to be one wild ride.

Every year we host thousands of visitors to the Dream Center. They look at the breadth of activities, the number of people involved, the towering 400,000-square-foot building that dominates our property, and the size of our budget and assume it has always been that way or that it emerged overnight. The truth is that the Dream Center began as a very tiny outreach to a little section of Los Angeles.

We began with a small church building and a couple of houses the church owned on an adjacent street. After my Echo Park encounter with God, I began intentionally reaching out to the neighbors right around our building. Soon a few people began showing up for services. We began to serve other people in various ways and rented out one house after another in the neighborhood as they were vacated, allowing us to house drug addicts in our recovery program. Just as we outgrew those buildings, we happened upon an abandoned fifteen-story hospital with eight adjacent buildings on a nine-acre campus that the Catholic church was selling. We didn't have the money, but God worked it out, giving us a large campus with room to grow. But then we outgrew the gymnasium on that campus, in which we were holding our worship services, and God worked out our merger with Angelus Temple, the historic building where the legendary Aimee Semple McPherson pastored.

The vision of the Dream Center today is to see thousands of hurting people come to know a new life through the efforts of our staff, volunteers, and the recently rehabilitated individuals whose lives have been dramatically changed. Whether it's by providing food, clothing, shelter, life rehabilitation, education, job training, or biblical training, we reach thousands of hurting and needy children, families, and adults across all races and cultures each week.

So in the past fifteen years, the cause God had given me in Echo Park had grown far beyond the little church I'd come to help restore. To celebrate this occasion, our inclination had been to throw a party to review all the great work we had done, a night during which we could escape the challenges and hardships of serving the poor, the distraught, the addicted, the sick, the abused.

But in the privacy of my heart that week, God grilled me like a prosecutor interviewing the accused in a courtroom trial: How can you abandon and reject the thing you love? How can you take credit for outcomes you were incapable of producing? How could you run from the very thing that has given you the greatest joy and fulfillment in your life?

Sometimes, I've found, you need to get radical to get right, to get back in touch with the very heartbeat of the cause that lies within you. My night on skid row was one of those times.

CHAPTER 3

SIDEWALK CELEBRATION

MY FIRST HOUR on the streets was the scariest sixty minutes of my life. I was terrified. The atmosphere is more frightening than anything you'd witness in a scary movie.

Once I arrived at the heart of skid row, I stopped in an effort to absorb it all. The sound of gunshots echoes through the streets. Yelling and screaming are common—drug addicts trying to kick the habit, alcoholics brawling in the street, prostitutes demanding their money, pimps beating their prostitutes to take away that money—it really is a war zone. I had arrived possessing an image of skid row as a place where anorexic, destitute people wandered aimlessly, looking for food and shelter, too frail or self-absorbed or scared to bother others. Wrong! The streets may be the best example of Darwinism, where the strong prey on the weak, and almost everyone is weak at some stage during their skid row sentence. I discovered very quickly that this was not merely an intriguing case study for sociologists to analyze and discuss. On this side of town, simply living to see the next day is a victory.

As my journey into the heart of hell began, some of Lawrence's warnings took on new meaning.

"Just be cool," he had warned, worried about my harebrained idea. "When you get there, just keep walking. They gonna surround you, look you over, smell you. They'll know you not from there. You can't hide it from them. They got a sixth sense about that. All they's worried about is if you some kinda threat to them—a cop or narc or bounty hunter. So you just keep walking, don't get into it with them. Just stay focused. Do your thing. When you ready to lay down and sleep, you find a good place and just sleep. Let them walk around you and stare at you, just keep livin' your life and don't bother nobody. And make sure you carry your Bible so they can see it."

"What?" I almost shouted, incredulous. "How am I supposed to fit in if I'm packing a Bible? I don't want them knowing I'm a pastor just coming in for a night or two. I want to fit in, be invisible. I need to feel what it's like to be homeless."

Lawrence paused before he respectfully replied. "Pastor Matthew, this ain't no game. It's dangerous on the street. You carry that Bible. The streets is mean, but they still got a reverence for the Word of God. A lot of them people is hurtin' out there, and deep down they know that God is their only hope. They don't go to church or Sunday school, but many of them got faith. In their mind, anybody totin' a Bible probably ain't lookin' for a fight, is probably not gonna be in their face. You don't have to preach, but the Word will be your protection. You carry that Bible."

And so it was that for the first hour, I kept my head down and just followed the trail of those in front of me, walking, walking, I didn't know where to, just staying in motion. I clutched my cardboard "mattress" in one hand and put my Bible under my arm. And just as Lawrence had promised, the street people were checking me out. It reminded me of a pack of dogs sniffing me, tracking my scent.

What I hadn't anticipated was the hum. As we all shuffled about, they looked me over and commented. "You don't belong here," one would say loudly, not quite a shout, but louder than normal—and then he'd move on, mumbling something unintelligible. The people who followed would be making some kind of noise under their breath, a hum, not melodic, but kind of chant-like, a bit chilling if you're not used to it. And then a minute or two later another guy would loudly inform me that I wasn't from there, I'd better get out, go back where I belong, and then he'd also continue his shuffling toward an undefined location, grumbling under his breath, adding to the street hum. I have to admit, I was praying for all I was worth during those first minutes.

Things got better when, almost by mistake, I put my Bible in my free hand. That immediately changed the game. It was remarkable. It was like a place of darkness in which a light was suddenly turned on. Even the pitch of the hum seemed to rise a note or two—maybe I imagined that, but it seemed to give the street a different tenor. Now that the Bible was visible, a few people stopped and asked questions about the Bible, my faith, or if I believed in God. It was a striking shift.

After the terror of that first hour wore off and I sensed that I could make it through the night, a strange peace settled over me. God was in this! I remained alert, still wary of what was happening around me, but my primary emotion shifted from fear to compassion. The Scripture came to mind that says perfect love casts out all fear.[1] As my heart was broken a bit more with each passing moment, realizing that what I was observing was the normal and full life experience for these hundreds of people strewn up and down these filthy, unforgiving streets, my love for them grew stronger.

They are my cause. They are the reason I get out of bed in the morning, the hope I have for making a difference in the world. I did not live there, but I belonged there. I was called to serve them.

Fear cannot own you when a great cause rules your heart. The fear

I'd felt just minutes ago had transitioned into a conviction that this was, indeed, where God wanted me—where God *needed* me, for my sake—to be tonight. It sure wasn't paradise. The stink of urine and body odor made me want to puke, the lighting was just dim enough

Fear cannot own you when a great cause rules your heart.

to be irritating, cigarette smoke billowed around me, constant yelling and incoherent speech filled my ears, the chaos of bodies moving everywhere toward nowhere was confusing.

Yet in the midst of this mind-numbing, logic-defying reality, I felt as if I was being broken and reborn all over again. That must be what I was here for—to stoke the embers of my passion for these people whom God loves so much that He gave His only Son to die on their behalf, for their future.[2] The title of Al Gore's book *An Inconvenient Truth* flashed through my mind; this was surely *an inconvenient life* on display throughout the streets of Los Angeles. But God is good, indeed. In the midst of the squalor and danger, He was giving me the gift of inconvenience so that I could become an ever more capable conduit of His love for this tribe of broken people.

Eventually I caught wind that if you arrived at the mission too late, there'd be no places left to sleep inside, so I joined a pack of people heading to one of the larger missions on the row. We got there, only to find out that the prime spaces were already filled up; the indoor beds were all taken for the night. They had an overflow area, a gymnasium, filled with chairs you could sleep in, sitting upright, but those, too, were taken. The only space left was in a large patio near the front of the mission property. It was outdoors, but it was a mild September night and at least the area was well-lit and had security guards posted. I headed there.

As I circled the inside of the patio area, sizing up my options, one of the security guys saw me and did a double take. He recognized me from church, but I gave him a look, and he caught on really quick. He was cool about it: he didn't give me away; he just gave me a faint grin and a little wink and kept up his rounds. I think he understood what I was doing, maybe even respected it. Anyway, he kept his eye on me while I was there. Another little blessing from God.

The concrete floor of the patio was jammed with bodies. There was a narrow pathway you could tread to snake your way through the courtyard, but otherwise it was body against body, all sorts of men and women trying to get some sleep in this sanctuary. It was late, and the emotional roller coaster of the evening was taking its toll on me; the energy I'd felt an hour ago had abandoned me, and now my feet were starting to ache and my energy was waning. I scanned the entire patio area, hoping to spy an undiscovered nook where I could sack out. All I saw was a little garden area a ways off, encircled by a cement bench. Nobody was on the far portion of the bench, so I lugged my cardboard over, set it down on the cement, and made myself as comfortable as possible. It felt good to get off my feet.

Within seconds, the guy to my right slid up against me and began talking nonstop. Nonstop and nonsense. I tried to follow his speech for a few minutes but found it too taxing. He was rambling about racism. His words reminded me how segregated skid row was—an alley might harbor a dozen people seeking sleep, but they'd all be of the same race or ethnicity. Blacks stuck with blacks, Hispanics with Hispanics, whites with whites. There weren't many Asians—at least I didn't encounter them. But the jumbled thoughts of my neighbor led me nowhere, and I tuned him out.

Unfortunately, his body was really hot, which made me uncomfortable, and his breath smelled of booze. I shifted a bit to create some space between us, only to bump up against the elderly fellow on my left. I took him to be a war veteran. His craggy face was covered with a gray beard, his thinning hair greasy under a ball cap. He was dozing off, but every few seconds he'd start shaking wildly, and groaning softly, as if he was having bad dreams about past war exploits.

I sat between these two, thinking again that these were people we could help. This whole room was filled with people who needed to be loved. And as I studied the faces and bodies strewn throughout the room, it felt like the Kingdom of God: people of all races, ages, and genders accounted for—a room full of broken people needing lots of practical love and genuine encouragement. Again I prayed that God would expand the boundaries of my love for His people and give me the strength to do what needed to be done. He brought to mind the thousands of people who have had their lives changed by the Dream Center. This could be our next wave of graduates. Their lives, too, would be changed someday by the love of God and His people. I sat back and smiled, oblivious to the ranting of the man on my right and the convulsions of the guy on my left. We'd be back to help them. I knew it.

I prayed that God would expand the boundaries of my love for His people and give me the strength to do what needed to be done.

After a couple of hours I returned to the streets, too curious to stay inside the safe confines of the mission. This was my chance to soak up all the sounds, sights, smells, and experiences that God had in store for me. Walking from street to street, I studied the nightlife on the row. Bonfires burned brightly on streets and in alleys as people huddled for warmth or to heat up morsels of food they'd saved up or had scavenged from Dumpsters.

As time dragged on—and the nights are agonizingly long on skid row—the noise level increased, and the intensity of the yelps and shouts rose too. More than once I jumped when a particularly startling shriek or wail burst forth. It was eerie. I don't think I have ever been so eager to see the sunrise.

Sometime between 3:00 and 4:00 a.m. I was standing under one of the streetlights when a voice emerged from the shadows of the driveway behind me. I felt no fear—more a curiosity to see whom God was placing in my path now. It was a man's voice. I could vaguely make out his silhouette against the brick wall of the building he was lying against. The only part of him that was in the light was his feet, caught under the edge of the light thrown by the streetlamp. He had sandals on his feet, and even in the imperfect light I could see how crusted and swollen his feet were. He did not sound drunk, just worn out. He had my attention, so he made his request.

"Hey, dude—man with the Bible. Come over here, man. Would you read a Scripture to me?"

I moved closer to him, and his other features came into view. I gazed up the rest of the driveway, which dead-ended about twenty feet farther up. The entire driveway was crammed with people sleeping this way and that, many on pieces of cardboard like mine, some huddled on the bare pavement.

I opened my Bible and smiled at the man. "What do you want to hear?" I asked, feeling a bit dizzy with the privilege of sharing this man's territory and the Word of God with him. He asked for something uplifting. I read a couple of psalms to him and added some words of encouragement. He thanked me.

After the second passage, someone farther up the driveway called to me from the dark. "Can I still be saved?" So direct! Maybe when your life could end at any moment, you get right to the point, no beating around the bush, no qualifiers, just wanting the bottom line. I spoke softly but confidently about the love of God, the forgiveness that He offers to all of us, that Jesus came so that nobody would have to die without the assurance of His unconditional love, how Jesus was the only hope that anyone in Los Angeles had, whether they lived in Beverly Hills or on skid row. Someone else from the opposite side of the alley guffawed and coughed out a response I couldn't make out. Undaunted, I reassured them that their lives were not hopeless, that God's love could get them through even the longest, darkest nights.

One man started pouring out his life story to me—to all of us, really—describing in agonized detail how much he missed his children but couldn't go home to see them because his former drug dealer would kill him if he ever returned home. He had failed to pay the dealer so he was forced to go into hiding. After a while he wound up, on skid row. His family didn't even know if he was still alive, but he knew that if he showed his face in his old neighborhood, he'd be a dead man. We talked back and forth about his options, his faith, his hope for the future. Others began chiming in, laying out the lurid details of their experiences, trying to find a connection with God, or truth, or hope, something that would make sense of it all. Their vulnerability—and their pain—touched me at a deep level.

Once the conversation died down, I laid my cardboard on the ground at the end of the driveway, at the edge of the light, and sought a nap. I needed a few minutes of rest. Homelessness is exhausting. Time seems to move more slowly than it does in the rest of the world. It was only a matter of seconds before I was asleep.

Sometime around 5:00 a.m. I was awakened by a tickling sensation. I scrunched up against the wall behind me and jerked my way into a sitting position, trying to figure out what was happening. Then it struck me—a cockroach was crawling up my left pant leg. I jumped up and shook myself, trying to free the little bugger from inside my clothing. It finally tumbled onto my sneaker, bounced onto the cement, then scurried away. That was gross!

Now awake—I mean full-on alert, after that little exercise—I figured I might as well move on. It was still pitch black, the urine smell was still overpowering—do you ever get used to it?—strange cries and unintelligible yelling were still puncturing the night air, bonfires still flickered here and there. And people were still moving up and down the streets, perhaps traveling a bit more slowly than earlier in the night, as fatigue caught up with those still on their feet. I retrieved my precious piece of cardboard, all soiled with grease and oil absorbed from the various pieces of ground I'd called home thus far that night, and resumed my own walk to oblivion.

Within a minute or so, a woman lurched toward me and quietly asked, "Hey, man, are you straight?" From conversations with guys in the rehab program at the Dream Center I knew that was a sexual come-on. Five in the morning on skid row, and the pastor gets propositioned for sex! I sighed, feeling so distraught for her; imagine what it takes to walk up to random men and ask if they'd like to buy her for a brief sexual interlude—and then having to make good on her end of the deal. My heart broke yet again.

As gently as I could, I told her no, I wasn't interested, I was a pastor, and showed her my Bible. All at once her demeanor changed—from the tough, in-control exterior to a look of sheer embarrassment. She backed up slowly, apologizing and asking me to forgive her. I advanced cautiously and tried to quell her fears, assuring her I was not offended, that I understood her predicament and wanted to help her. She looked at me and a tear came down her face and she sobbed through her story, explaining that she was just selling herself to get money for the drugs she needed, that her life was a mess, and she was going through a really hard time. I told her that if she was serious about getting her life together, I could help. I could call our team at the church and have someone there at 7:00 a.m. to pick her up and bring her back to the Dream Center, where she could get help to kick her habit and get her life back on track. I waited for her permission to make the call.

She looked at her watch, then scrunched up her face, looking at me like I was crazy. It took me a moment to figure out that she thought I was scamming her. No church was open at 5:00 a.m., ready to have someone on-site at 7:00 a.m. just to help her. I smiled, realizing how unusual our ministry is, but explained that we're a 24-7 church because people's needs don't respect the clock. We talked for a few minutes, and she wept through her admission of how badly she wanted to kick her habit. Without much prodding, she agreed to enter our drug rehab program, so I called our team and arranged for a bus to be there for her at 7:00. We exchanged cell numbers, and I passed her number on to the ministry team.

I'd been praying all night that the Lord would give me somebody to help, and then He delivered Annette to me. We parted ways, but I called her a couple of times before 7:00 a.m. to encourage her to be there, to be sure she'd show up at the pick-up spot. She kept promising to be there. A lot of times people chicken out—they want the help and know how badly they need it, but they just can't take that first step, so I kept calling her so she wouldn't lose her nerve.

Sure enough, at 7:00 a.m., she came striding down the street, a determined look on her face. I hugged her, thanked her for her courage and integrity, and introduced her to our team members on the bus. She boarded it as I promised to check in on her later in the week.

Meanwhile, the streets continued to pulsate with action and danger.

Finally, daylight made its appearance, and the swarm of activity that filled the streets on the row vanished. The fires flickered out. The yelling ceased, or maybe it was just less noticeable once the noise of the cars and city buses took over. Many of the people who'd shared alley space with me seemed to have a daily routine they fell into—going from mission to mission, getting their daily needs met by the organizations that dispense compassion to the down-and-out who are captives of the inner city. I talked to a few street people, gathering intelligence about options, and put together a schedule to follow for the day.

After getting breakfast at one of the missions and then engaging several homeless folks in conversations about their lives, I prepared to try my luck at panhandling. This was the part of the exercise I dreaded the most—begging for money—but I was committed to giving it a shot, to discover what this task was like.

During my endless night I'd thought about how to do this. I figured there were two keys to success. One was staking out a good location. I'd heard real estate brokers say that it's all about where you are—location, location, location. To receive money, I'd have to go where the money was—and that certainly meant leaving skid row for a while. Stationing myself in the central business district seemed to make the most sense. It was an area that would allow me to hit up the impeccably dressed, purposeful executives who frequented those blocks. So after wolfing down another free meal, a pretty reasonable lunch from one of our church's teams—I knew the schedule and where they'd be, so I took advantage of the opportunity to see our people in action and test the quality of our food—I walked out of the poverty zone and into the heart of corporate America, not sure what to expect.

The second key to success, in my mind, was my story. What would I tell people? I didn't want to lie, but I wasn't exactly a hard-luck case, either. So I crafted a carefully worded tale about how times were tough and I just needed a little bit to help get me going. I didn't have any money, I wanted something to eat, and I'd be grateful for any change you could spare. All of that was true. Armed with that story, I felt I could approach people with conviction.

Now, I don't want to brag, but I was doing really well at this. I made $7 in my first half hour. I mean, that's just about better than what I make per hour at the church! Well, not really, but it feels that way sometimes.

Anyway, this was truly an eye-opening—and gut-wrenching—experience. The mere memory of it makes me queasy. Listen, I've been criticized by the best of them—called out for my preaching, my leadership, my theology, my age, my education, you name it—and I've learned the hard way that getting blasted by one's peers is just part of the game, a reflection of professional jealousy or doctrinal disagreement or whatever. But none of the criticism I've received as a pastor wounded me as deeply as what I experienced on the streets that afternoon while asking for money.

The most amazing part of my panhandling effort was the total rejection and scorn I experienced from so many people. Having been on the receiving end of countless pitches for funds by street people, I knew that a beggar's request was an uncomfortable intrusion into people's lives. But the hatred and disgust with which many people responded was both unexpected and debilitating. There were moments during this brief phase of my skid row adventure when I felt it was time to quit and go home to my nice house and loving family. This cut too deeply.

"You want *my* money? Why don't you get a job and earn it? That's how I got it."

"Hey, get away from me. And leave me alone."

Every human being has the right to basic dignity, but the disdain heaped on me by people from whom I was simply seeking help or understanding chipped away at it. It was hard enough to muster the courage to approach total strangers and throw myself on their mercy, realizing that if I did not have a better situation to return to, this would be part of my daily fate, a crucial component of my survival. To receive looks that left no doubt I was a vile, even evil person pierced my already-broken heart and battered my self-image.

"Bug off, you bum. And get out of this area—people who work for a living have things to do here. Go rot on your side of town."

"Don't touch me, dirtbag. Make better choices if you want a different life."

In all fairness, there were some kind and gracious people who showed some degree of care toward me and either forked over some change or had an uplifting word for me. You cannot imagine the hope such behavior ignited within me—the hope that maybe I wasn't the pond scum some had suggested, that perhaps I could make it through the tough times—and even deserved to. Believe me, after even a half hour of asking strangers for help, you question your self-worth and reason for living.

My short-lived panhandling experience may well have been so emotionally disturbing because of my own ambivalence about panhandlers—wanting to help them but not wanting to give superficial assistance that merely perpetuates their resistance to real help. From firsthand experience I know that every single person living on those streets can be restored to health and their own dream can be pursued, realistically and purposefully. That's what the Dream Center is all about—and we have several thousand case studies to prove it can be done, whether the person is a multimillionaire with an empty heart or a frail, alcoholic prostitute with an empty stomach. But that afternoon I was being schooled in why it is so hard for some people to take that first step toward acknowledging and embracing their dream and risking what little self-respect they have left in order to pursue it. I could not remember ever feeling more depressed—or stripped of dignity.

If things seemed bad at the time, they were about to get worse. As I moved from one location to another in an effort to hit up as many different kinds of people as possible, a uniformed security guard rushed out of one of the marble-faced buildings I was in front of. He angrily and loudly told me to get away from their building. I meekly explained that I was just trying to get some money for food. He launched into a tirade about how my intrusion on their property was an act of terrorism—*terrorism*, for goodness' sake!—and that the public has laws protecting them from people like me, and so forth. It was quite a performance. His spiel attracted more than a few gawkers, making me feel even worse. Then he threatened to have me arrested.

No matter how much I wanted to learn about living on the streets and to feel the reality of that lifestyle, going to jail wasn't on my to-do list for the day. I could envision the headline in tomorrow's *Los Angeles Times*: "Disheveled Megachurch Pastor Arrested for Harassing Businesspeople While Soliciting Funds." I didn't even want to imagine the stories that would run in Christian periodicals. I moved on without any further struggle.

While retreating from that area with the hostile glares of passersby and the combative words of the security guard deposited into my memory bank, I noticed the video cameras attached to the building that were doubtless following the scene. In a moment of illumination I realized that if you are exposed to enough of this kind of demeaning treatment, day after day, it probably becomes a self-fulfilling prophecy: you begin to believe that all these important, successful people must be right; you are a worthless piece of human trash, void of hope, living for nothing.

A couple of blocks from that scene, I stopped and leaned against a brick column in front of one of the mega-story buildings. Dozens of people rushed by me as if I were invisible—or maybe they just wanted me to be. I felt lower than ever—and knew that God was responding to my request to break my heart anew for the poor and defenseless, to give me a bigger capacity to love and heal them through His power and authority. At that moment, though, all I felt was despair and crushing defeat. As that building held me up, I closed my eyes and thanked God for this experience and asked for the strength and zeal to address people's needs more adeptly.

If I'd ever had any doubt about the magnitude of the need, my brief stint panhandling erased it. And if there was ever any thought that the impact of the Dream Center was attributable to me, this episode destroyed that delusion. The depth of these issues could only be overcome by God-sized love delivered by Him alone. My colleagues and I were simply privileged to be instruments He used in the process.

The night before, prior to leaving the van and touching down on the streets, I had decided I would stay until I felt spiritually full, whether that took a few hours, a day, or maybe until just before having to return to my church to preach on Sunday morning.

I reached that sense of completion right around sundown. I'd only been there twenty-two hours, but it seemed to have lasted for an eternity. Now I was anxious to get back to the Dream Center and share all that I had learned. It was time to inject a new level of enthusiasm and energy into our efforts to restore the dreams and hope of the broken, discarded lives in Los Angeles. God had accomplished what He wanted and what I'd prayed for: a renewed sense of vision that hopefully would propel us into another fifteen years of vigorous and compassionate service to the forgotten souls of society, providing a reflection of His love with warmth, grace, and wisdom.

I called the team back at the office and asked them to send the van to come get me. While waiting for my ride, I somberly reviewed the ironies of the past day. Initially I'd felt afraid of the very people I was called to love. I was being broken alongside the broken people I wanted to heal. I had sought insight and understanding from those I hoped to educate and train for a better life experience. I had been driven to the streets by the excitement of the possibilities before completely comprehending the personal risk associated with the experience.

It dawned on me that over the course of time, as we pursue the cause that God has placed within us, we unknowingly reshape that dream to satisfy our personal comfort level. The more time and energy we devote to the cause within us, the more likely we are to lose touch with the heartbeat of the original cause, redefining it according to our current desires, circumstances, needs, plans, and goals.

One of the greatest benefits from my day on the streets was that it restored the original contours of God's dream for me—contours that had been slowly, imperceptibly replaced by my version of the dream. Hanging out on skid row had been dangerous and scary, yes, but embracing that risk was necessary to be personally broken and freed to do what God had called me to do.

My day on the streets restored the original contours of God's dream for me—contours that had been slowly, imperceptibly replaced by my version of the dream.

One night earlier I had gone to skid row hoping that God would give me new insights into how to change people. Instead, God changed me—and impressed upon me again the reality that I cannot change people, only He can, but if my heart is right He may be willing to use me in the process.

I went to skid row with a secret thought that what I was doing was somehow heroic. I left there knowing that I was not a hero but a servant.

The night before, I had hit the streets feeling I was entering a danger zone. Returning to the Dream Center, I realized the real danger was living a routine life not fully aligned with God's cause for me.

Do you know the cause God has instilled in your heart, the opportunity that represents the very reason for your life? He has such a cause—call it a vision, a dream, a purpose, whatever term you like—for every one of us. And I want to tell you some stories about the people I've gotten to know who have discovered, as I have, that until you live for that cause, your life has not and cannot reach its potential. Let's figure out how to bring that God-given cause to the forefront of your life so you can experience the joy and fulfillment of changing the world by living the life you were meant to live.

CHAPTER 4

THE REASON TO GET OUT OF BED

IF YOU'RE LIKE most people I meet, you have at least a general sense of what your life is supposed to be about. You may see yourself as an educator, an organizer, a protector, or a manager. Ever since I was a teenager, I've known I was called to be a spiritual leader, just like my father and grandfather who served for many years as pastors of churches. But having a general sense of purpose doesn't really give you or me much of the detail regarding what it will look like in practice.

And that's where understanding the cause within you comes into play.

Surveys tell us that tens of millions of people—nearly half of all adults—admit they are still seeking to understand the meaning and ultimate purpose of their lives. Research confirms that a huge majority of people—more than three out of every four adults—say they want to make a difference in the world; they want their lives to count for some lasting, positive outcome. But the statistics further point out that most people hold on to that hope as something they may experience in the future; it is not a present reality for them. In other words, many of us do not know the cause that will give our lives genuine fulfillment.

When you were born, God instilled many things within you. One of them was a great cause that He wants you to embrace. In His unique grandeur, He created a universe in which the cumulative effect of all people faithfully pursuing the cause within them would result in a transformed world—one in which everyone's needs would be met and every servant's heart would be filled with the joy of blessing others. Unfortunately, we live in a traumatized world—in part because so many people fail to identify and pursue the cause He has given them. Even though it would provide the happiness and fulfillment they have been seeking, they have failed to build their lives around that cause.

A transforming cause is never about you. It is always about using the resources God has given you to make a positive impact in the lives of others.

From the outset, let me point out that I don't know the details of the great cause residing within you, but I do know that it is related to people—specifically, how you can make the world a better place by serving other people, whether one-on-one or behind the scenes. A transforming cause is never about you—promoting yourself, achieving greater fame or fortune, experiencing more pleasure or comfort, amassing greater power. It is always about using the resources God has given you—skills, relationships, experiences, money, time, intelligence, and all the rest—to make a positive impact in the lives of others.

To grasp that cause, your spirit needs to be awakened. So many people are alive but not really living—they're just surviving. That's *not* how it's meant to be! I get such inspiration from the ordinary people I meet who are doing extraordinary things because they have devoted themselves to the great cause God has custom designed just for them. They have had to search deep inside themselves and examine the information, people, experiences, and opportunities that God brought into their lives to discover how to get the most out of life. When they figured it out and committed themselves to that cause, they found that God partners with them in amazing ways. At the Dream Center, we see God doing miracles all the time—miracles that were made possible by ordinary people, like you and me, stepping up and stepping out to do astounding acts of service that really do change the world.

Sometimes people challenge this claim and say, "I can't do anything great. I don't have an education." Or, "My life is a mess. I have been physically and emotionally abused. I'm not strong enough to help others; I can barely help myself." Or, "I'm so busy right now, raising my children, trying to make ends meet financially, and taking care of my spouse; I just don't have the time or energy to change the world." Or even, "I'm not interested in helping other people. It's a dog-eat-dog world, and I've got to look out for myself. Nobody else will."

At the risk of offending you, let me point out that excuses like these are arrogant. Such statements betray that you are living by one of two fallacies: either you are fixated only on what you can do in your own strength, or you believe the only way to maximize your life is to focus on and take care of yourself. Such statements suggest that you believe living a successful life is all about who you see yourself to be, what you are able to do with your natural talent and ability, and when you feel ready to do something great.

On the one hand, you don't give God enough credit—not enough to believe that He would never set you up for *failure*, that He *wants* you to optimize your earthly journey, and that He *loves* you so much that He is eagerly awaiting the chance to partner with you to have an amazing impact in the lives you are able to touch. On the other hand, you're giving yourself too much credit. Sure, you can make choices, but ultimately you are not really in control of your place in the world; God is.

So don't settle for weak excuses about your inabilities, lack of experience, fear, busyness, personal needs, or other obstacles. Those are all distractions from the truth. We have had literally thousands of people come through the Dream Center who were addicted, abused, prostituted, abandoned, disabled—you name it, we've seen it. In spite of such barriers, many of those people transcended their challenges and limitations by choosing to trust God, getting their lives right, adopting a realistic perspective about life, and pursuing the cause He instilled within them. It's never easy—there is *always* a price to pay—but people invariably testify that their commitment to the cause elevated their life to a new level of significance and satisfaction. And there is a hidden benefit in being true to their cause. In every case, we hear our Dream Center volunteers explain that although their motivation was to help others, they feel as if they were the ones who had been helped the most.

In earlier chapters, I painted a pretty dark picture of life on the streets. Yet one person I met that night stood out because of the joy and hope she brought to the streets. This woman, I'm convinced, has found her cause.

Not long after midnight that evening, a flatbed truck pulled up to the curb a half block from where I was hanging out. It was a food truck, bringing the leftovers from a restaurant. Dozens of tacos, tortillas, quesadillas, and other Mexican specialties were handed out by the small group of workers on the flatbed. I waited in line, wondering if there'd be enough to go around. When I got to the front of the line, a Hispanic woman on the truck handed me a plate with something I couldn't make out in the dark, along with some beans on the side.

I smiled and thanked the woman for taking the time to help us and for being so generous. What happened next stunned me.

She looked into my eyes, jumped off the truck, and came alongside me. She threw her arm around me and said in a heavily accented, soothing voice, "Sir, don't worry, it's all going to be all right. You're going to make it through. Enjoy the food." She smiled, hopped back on the flatbed, and continued to serve others.

Man, did that get my emotions going—not embarrassment or sadness, but rekindling my own sense of compassion for these people. How inspiring this restaurant worker was, love oozing out of her, taking an extra few moments to console a stinky, dirty person she'd never met with a few heartfelt words of encouragement. Here it was, past midnight, yet she and her coworkers from the restaurant ignored their own fatigue, packaged up the extra food, drove to a dangerous area of the city, and took another half hour to hand out their excess. There were no TV cameras to record it, no nonprofit agencies on hand to give them a tax-deductible receipt. They were just quietly loving the poor. My heart burst with joy over their unheralded act of kindness.

With a twinge of pride I thought of the numerous teams of Dream Center volunteers who minister down here every week. Energized, I started thinking about ways we could expand our efforts downtown: run additional buses to pick up more of these poor people, add a new program for some of the sick ones who had no place to go for treatment, motivate more volunteers to come down here, raise more money to help greater numbers of these hurting and forgotten souls.

I was no longer fatigued; my strength had been renewed. This is what it's all about! I stood on the sidewalk and did a slow 360, panning the area and promising myself that those of us from the Dream Center would be back here day after day, more strategically and more boldly than ever. These people were not society's problems;

they had problems that society could solve—that the church, God's people, could solve. Through Jesus Christ we can solve all of these problems.

The engine of the flatbed truck roared to life. I turned to wave good-bye to the restaurant workers who had served us. They got it. They weren't just making and selling Mexican food. They were changing the world. They were living the Kingdom life.

Life is much simpler than we make it.

God's objective is for you to live an outward-looking life—that is, not worried about yourself, but focused on the needs of others and how you can respond to those needs. When you embrace that mind-set, you are on the precipice of influence and success because that's a perspective that God will bless. As soon as you start thinking about the needs and burdens of others, and what you can do to alleviate them, or how you can bless and build up others, you begin to establish a new identity for yourself—your true identity.

> **It doesn't take a person with unusual ability to change the world. All it takes is a heart that cares, a mind that's determined, a spirit that's willing, a cause that matters, and a person to help.**

It doesn't take a person with unusual training or ability to change the world. All it takes is a heart that cares, a mind that's determined, a spirit that's willing, a cause that matters, and a person to help.

When I arrived in Los Angeles as a twenty-year-old kid, I didn't appear to have much to offer—an opinion I quickly came to embrace. Yet in the midst of my despair, God led me to Echo Park. There He told me, *If you reach the people that nobody wants, I'll send you the people that everybody wants.*

At that moment, I had no idea—absolutely none—what serving

and blessing people in this place might entail or look like. I knew God would make that clear at the right time, though. At last I truly understood my cause. It was not to build a great church; it was to build great people. I set aside my personal, long-held plan—the church-building plan—and accepted the cause He had chosen for me.

To seal the deal that night, I got up and walked over to a pair of guys sitting on the curb, one of whom was in a lip-lock with Jack Daniel's, the other busy showing his mastery of vodka. I engaged them in casual conversation. They were open enough. I learned a few things. Before moving on, I thanked them for their time and told them about our church and even invited them to join me there during the coming week or next Sunday morning. They assured me they'd be there. I knew they were not likely to remember even speaking to me, much less show up, but this was feeling right. God was already instilling genuine love and compassion for these people in my heart. I felt no fear or disdain, only a sense of finally being on the right path toward making a difference with my life.

I learned a number of things about the cause within me that night in Echo Park. One of the biggest lessons was the importance of accepting God's load and releasing my own. For years there had been pressure and tension building up inside my head and heart over the challenge of building a great church. That was going to be my masterpiece, my magnificent gift to God. And then I found out He didn't even want it! Or maybe He was simply pointing out that nobody can build a great church for Him; only He can accomplish that feat. My real calling was to build great people. That wasn't my choice; it was His assignment for me. Because of that I could relax a bit and count on Him giving me the help I needed to accomplish the task.

When I was focused on building a great church, it was a heavy burden. It kept getting heavier because of all the requirements that were accumulating: all the tasks, functions, demands to meet, things to learn, people to manage, solutions to create, issues to understand, resources to secure, and so on. Every day, it seemed, added more weight to my dream of what it would take to build a great church. That explains why, at the age of twenty, I had ulcers already! My stomach was tied up in knots because the burden was simply too much.

But the beauty of the cause God gives you is that it is tailor-made for you. Like the Scripture says, His yoke is light and the burden easy to bear.[3] That's because your cause will utilize the strengths He has endowed you with. In recent years one of the emphases of businesses has been to identify a person's strengths and find ways to take advantage of those above-average capabilities. God gives you particular strengths, and your best bet is to invest yourself in exploiting them—ideally for His purposes. When you do what you're great at, it's not a strain; it's fun and invigorating. God wants you to enjoy serving others. That happens when you operate in your areas of strength. When you carry His load, it is light, especially in comparison to the burdens you create for yourself.

Here's the image I carry in my mind of how this works: when I start to feel overwhelmed, it's because I am heaping unproductive burdens on my shoulders; all I am doing is accumulating more commitments that do not facilitate positive results. But when I am fulfilling the cause that God gave me, I am continually giving to others, depleting the weight of whatever I have accumulated for the journey. The more I give, the lighter I feel. Sometimes, when I have given all I can give in that situation, I feel as light as a feather. I'm tired, sure, but I am exhilarated because I gave it all away and it's making a positive difference in someone else's life. It gives me a light-headed feeling, an unburdened feeling.

What experiences have lightened your load? I'll bet they are the kinds of efforts that display your gifts and abilities in situations where you are improving somebody else's life. And I'll bet those efforts are closely related to the cause that lies within you, waiting to be released and fulfilled.

One of the most important things that God reiterated during my coming-out party at Echo Park was that a cause is always about serving other people. I've read some of the popular books that talk about vision. Some of the vision statements that people and organizations pursue strike me as inaccurate because they focus on size (being the biggest), money (return on investment, wealth accumulation, shareholder value), reputation (universal name recognition, having an image as the best), position (winning a specific job title or achieving significant corporate standing), or satisfaction (pleasure or comfort received). Those are not necessarily bad things, and they may even be necessary components in fulfilling one's true cause. But they are not the embodiment or central reflection of the cause itself.

God loves people. He is not that interested in our bigness, wealth, popularity, or supremacy. He is interested in our relationship with Him and our relationship with people. In fact, Jesus summarized the purpose of our lives when He was debating the religious leaders of His day. "Love the LORD your God with all your heart, all your soul, all your mind, and all your strength . . . Love your neighbor as yourself."[4] Love is not just a feeling; it's more of a commitment. So your cause is to love people through your commitment to knowing and understanding them and through taking care of their needs. In other words, serve them.

Think about what that means. As an individual, your cause is somehow related to marrying your own passions, interests, and abilities with the needs of people. When are you most fulfilled? When you get to do what you're best at, what you enjoy the most, and what produces a meaningful difference in people's lives. Fulfilled artists do not paint or sculpt for the sake of creating more art. They do it to move people and challenge them to see the world differently. Competent teachers do not dispense information for the sake of distributing more facts or showing off their own knowledge. They teach in order to shape students' ability to think and solve problems, which prepares them for success in life. Policemen do not pull over reckless drivers to flaunt their authority or to meet a quota for the month. They do so to protect innocent people and to motivate reckless drivers to get their behavior under control, which makes the world a safer and thus better place.

Is it possible for artists, teachers, parents, police officers—or any of us—to lose sight of how our choices best serve the needs of others? Absolutely! But when we do things that are selfish, such as performing a task to the lowest level of ability just to get it done or doing something that makes *me* look good at the expense of my team, the ultimate outcome is inferior to what it could have been. In our culture today we often are tempted, if not encouraged, to do what's best to satisfy immediate, selfish, personal desires. We operate in the short term at the expense of lasting results. We magnify personal gain over our communal responsibility. What we wind up with is a society in which every person sees others either as competition or obstacles, rather than as recipients to be served. People become commodities that are simply a means through which we gain satisfaction. In other words, we get what America has become in the past quarter century.

There is only one antidote to that downhill slide: getting our eyes off ourselves and recognizing our inner cause, which calls us to take care of each other. We ultimately receive pleasure and fulfillment from doing so. But more than that, given the stated purpose of life—to love God and love others—it is simply the right thing to do. We can talk all we want about making a difference in the world, leaving the world a better place, imprinting our mark on the world, having a lasting legacy—but unless our core objective relates to ways in which we serve people to the best of our abilities, it's all just empty talk.

And it's not like serving is such a hardship. Many people seem to think that if you're helping others, you're sacrificing all the good things in life and acting as a do-gooder. That's not the case at all. When you find that sweet spot that reflects your cause, it is at the intersection of your passion (what really matters to you), your gifts (what you do best), and your contribution (how you make the world better). If you have identified your cause and invested yourself in it, you know what I'm talking about. If you haven't—well, you're in for the most pleasant surprise of your life. Serving is not all struggle and drudgery, although there may be some hardships involved. The fulfillment of your cause will leave things better than you found them—and that includes you.

One of the pleasant discoveries I made over the years is that when you serve others, the impact of your service keeps rippling out further and further, affecting more people than you will ever realize. A great example is our Adopt-A-Block program at the Dream Center. It's the simplest of activities, but it has an unbelievable ripple effect. Adopt-A-Block involves a team of people committing to visit the same city block every week. Every Saturday the team knocks on the door of each home on the block, asking the residents if there is anything they can do to serve them and offering to pray with them when they're ready to leave. Then they move to the next door and repeat the process.

The fulfillment of your cause will leave things better than you found them—and that includes you.

We now have hundreds of people joining us every Saturday to visit their adopted blocks and serve each household they visit however they can. (Of course, one of the biggest ways we help residents is simply by befriending them and letting them know they matter and are loved by someone who expects nothing in return.) We presently assist more than 30,000 people every weekend, providing all kinds of help: food, clothing, plumbing, electrical repairs, medical assistance, painting, gardening, homework help, and so forth. (We have volunteers with specialized skills—e.g., plumbing, electrical work, medical care—on call to go wherever their specialty is needed.) Often we are the only people to visit an elderly or ill person during the week, and they look forward to having our people come by and encourage them.

Sometimes when I meet people from other areas of Los Angeles, they start talking to me as if we've known each other for years. As we get into it, I discover that they have relatives living on one of our adopted streets and are familiar with what we do on those blocks. They'll ask, "When are you coming to my neighborhood?" and rave about how wonderful we are and what a difference our teams make in our adopted neighborhoods. It struck me that our little acts of love have a ripple effect. People who don't even attend our church are proud of it because they appreciate the unconditional love we offer. And that has opened up many opportunities for us to do even more acts of service and reach greater numbers of people with the love of God, sharing His redemptive love with people when they are ready to receive it.

In the course of my travels I meet people who say they don't like God or they don't like Christian churches. That's okay with me, because I have come to find that they don't really hate God or churches; they hate a false impression they have of what God or churches are like.

It's always a joy to introduce such people to those at the Dream Center because the passion, energy, and enthusiasm of our people just blow their minds. In a quick walk across our property, you'll meet toothless people who never finished grade school and people with PhDs in subjects I can't even pronounce. The thread they have in common is a need to be loved and the joy of serving. Once they've identified and committed to their causes, their lives are no longer their own; they are devoted to loving God by serving others.

My encounters with the God-haters are a blast because I know what's coming. They start off with stories about the uncaring nature of God, or the atrocities committed in His name, or how they don't believe He even exists. And then they meet some of our people.

What the naysayers learn is that God is not a distant being who dispenses rules and punishment. He is love, and His love has transformed those He loves, who then act as a conduit for His love through their service to others. The doubters see firsthand that God revels in giving cause-driven people a great adventure for life, one that stirs them like no other motivation can. They see that true faith is an active faith—not just a lot of head knowledge from sermons and Bible classes, but a way of living that embraces a mission of changing the world for the better through the power of God. They listen to the testimonies of rehabilitated drug addicts, or girls who were rescued from sex trafficking, or poor families who live for free on our campus while they get their lives back together, or emancipated teenagers who are getting an education so they can survive and thrive in the world. Before you know it, they realize that what they are hearing about are genuine miracles. And then they begin to understand that there really is a God who loves us and wants to work with us in loving others. The turnaround in the attitude of many of the doubters is amazing—another little miracle in itself.

My assistant, Todd, is a great example of this transition. He shifted from not believing in God to being intrigued by the selfless efforts of God's people to eventually accepting and embracing Jesus to becoming a servant himself. Todd was raised as a nominal Jew but morphed into a practicing atheist. He had a very responsible job managing a couple of theaters in Los Angeles, including the El Capitan Theater in Hollywood. (That's an old, majestic theater where Disney launches their new family movies and provides a special, hands-on experience related to the film.) A couple of his friends brought him to one of our church services. He had never been in a church in his life and did not know that Jesus Christ was a real person. He knew next to nothing about Christianity, even though he grew up right here in the LA area.

The first time he came to our church, we had a special service where Jim Bakker, the former televangelist, was speaking to our congregation. Jim has a remarkable story of his own experience with the Dream Center; I'll get to that later. Anyway, Jim finished speaking, and my dad and I were onstage crying over Jim's words, hugging him and welcoming him to our congregation. And Todd was sitting in the audience, perplexed by who all these strange men onstage were, who were hugging each other and crying in front of hundreds of people. Todd tells his story best:

> I had absolutely no idea what was going on, who these people were, and what in the world I was doing there. But I felt something I'd never felt before in my life. There I was in this strange church with these unusual people all around me, trying to figure out what was going on. But I had that feeling. So I came back with my friends the following Sunday. And then I came back Thursday and then the following Sunday again. It wasn't easy for me, being in my midthirties and with my beliefs set.
>
> I have a scientific kind of mind, one that loves facts and figures. But a lot of the Bible stories I was hearing didn't make sense to me. People having babies at a hundred years old? I don't think so. A guy living in a big fish's mouth for several days? No. I mean, this stuff just made no sense. So it took me several months of coming back, listening, watching these people, before any of it started to make sense. But

I kept coming back—always with my two friends, who I trusted, because the rest of these Christians kinda scared me. They were weird. They liked to sing with their arms waving in the air and stuff like that. Who were these people? Where did they come from?

One night I was walking out after the service, and a woman came up to me and asked, "Are you going to Pastors School?" And I was thinking, *Why would I do that? I'm not a pastor.* I wasn't even saved yet. So I simply said no. And just after I walked out the back door of the church, I felt this really strong impression: *turn around, go back inside, sign up for Pastors School.* It made no sense, but it seemed right, so I did it. I was probably the only atheist in a room full of pastors for several days learning how to be a better pastor.

Through a set of odd circumstances, Todd not only traveled to Phoenix for the pastor's conference held annually at my dad's church, but he wound up staying in my hotel room for the three nights, so we got to know each other. During those few days he not only attended the teaching sessions, but he also helped me shop for a shirt and tie to wear for the session I was leading (he didn't like my taste in ties), ironed my entire suit (something I neither asked for nor expected), and even helped at the table where we were selling CDs by our music team, which played during the conference. After we returned to Los Angeles from that event, Todd really got engaged with what we do:

When we were in Phoenix, I again felt that same voice inside of me, and I knew, somehow, that I was being called to serve this man, Matthew Barnett, and the amazing vision he had for LA. While we were in Phoenix, I got saved and made the decision to quit my job and begin to serve Matthew and work with the others attached to the Dream Center. I had never felt anything so strongly before in my life.

We came back to LA, and I immediately started studying everything spiritual. I was doing personal research projects on different Scriptures. There's one passage in the book of Hebrews that talks about whether man is created a little higher or lower than angels,[5] and I dove into it and wrote a twenty-seven-page research paper on it. It was a pretty thorough piece, describing how some biblical scholars translate that passage to say angels are higher, while others translate it to say people are higher.

When I finished the paper, I gave it to Pastor Matthew and told him how hard I'd worked on it and presented both sides of the argument. I told him I wanted him to tell me which it was: are we higher or lower than angels? He looked at me and said, "Who cares? Who does this help? Whose life does this change?" And I said I didn't know. He said, "Nobody, that's who! No one. Zero people. You know what you need to do with this? Get rid of it and go out and feed some hungry people. Then if you still need to know the answer to that question, ask Jesus after you die. For now, that stuff doesn't matter. Find someone to help and take care of their needs." That's what I needed to hear at that stage in my process. So I became a one-year volunteer, quitting my job at the theater and everything.

In my first month at the Dream Center, the director of security talked to me and mentioned that Pastor Matthew needed to be protected when he went out visiting people on this new outreach among homeless people living under the freeway overpasses. They called it Under the Bridge because that's where we'd go meet with them, right where they were living, under the bridges. It's a staple in our ministry now, but it was brand-new then. I didn't know anything about it, but I agreed to go. Let me tell you, meeting and working with those people through Under the Bridge was one of the things that really transformed my life. On my first weekend I hugged a guy with hepatitis C. I mean, I had never even hugged a dirty person before that! He was a really skinny guy, and he died about a week later.

When you go out there and see the people's needs, it breaks your heart. I did Under the Bridge for a while, then eventually did Adopt-A-Block for years and years. You're forever changed. It's the best way to catch the vision and to see beyond yourself. Go out, see the need, serve someone. You'll never be the same. I've been doing this for thirteen years now. I learned that anything is possible through God, and anyone can be reached. But they are reached by people like you and me.

Your cause is an exciting mission that God is sending you on. It transcends the mundane challenges of earning a living or surviving the usual daily crises. Your cause is the engine that will make your world turn. It's more stimulating than anything else you face. It's not about being religious. It's all about being a servant.

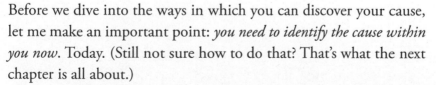

Before we dive into the ways in which you can discover your cause, let me make an important point: *you need to identify the cause within you now*. Today. (Still not sure how to do that? That's what the next chapter is all about.)

The quicker you get busy pursuing your cause, the faster you'll experience the fulfillment and joy it produces. The sooner you make progress toward satisfying your cause, the sooner you will begin to change the world, a little bit at a time, but eventually adding up to a serious impact. The more you immerse yourself in the cause—thinking about it, doing it, enjoying it—the more momentum it builds. Then your impact really snowballs. You're adding value to the world. You're not just a resource extractor; you become an agent of growth and a provider of benefits. Test it; you'll find it doesn't get better than that. And once you get your cause rolling and the momentum builds, it's like being in the front seat of a roller coaster: fast, furious, fearless, and fun!

When God made you, in addition to the cause He placed within you, He also gave you a lot of other good qualities. Pursuing your cause is the best way to empty yourself of all those good characteristics. That's a viable goal for life: use yourself up, doing good wherever you can, until you've got nothing left to give. When you're empty, then you can die happy because of all the positive outcomes you've facilitated and all the ways God has been able to work through you to change the world. Sometimes you will think you're on the brink of emptiness and have nothing more to offer. Just then, God will fill you up again, and the ride can continue. But first you have to get going, and today is the best opportunity you'll ever have to begin living the ultimate life.

Are you ready? This will be a life-changer for you. Let's take a practical walk through the process of making your life count for all it can be. In the chapters that follow, I want to explore these aspects of the cause within you:

- Finding your great cause
- Overcoming the inevitable obstacles related to leading a cause-focused life
- Preparing to make the most of your cause-related opportunities
- Making a personal commitment to the cause

- Getting the job done
- Working in partnership with others
- Persevering through the dry times and the down cycles
- Experiencing the pleasures and rewards of living for your God-given cause
- Reveling in the peace with God that's fostered by your cause

Still not sure if this is a journey you want to take? Here's my offer for you to consider: Give it ninety days of honest effort. Pour yourself into the process, and practice like you really believe in it and want to make it work. If pursuing the cause within you fails to turn your crank after ninety days of sincere effort, then give it up. Find something else to live for, something that proves to be better than serving people through your passion and strengths. I cannot even begin to imagine what that would be; I'm completely confident that you'll find living for your cause gives new meaning and energy to your life. But like the Bible says, don't take my word for it; test it.[6] If it's good, you win; stick with it and enjoy it. If it falls flat, you haven't lost much—only a brief amount of time and energy during which you'll undoubtedly learn something about yourself and others that will be fruitful in your future endeavors.

WHAT I'VE LEARNED
- Everyone has a God-given cause designed specifically for him or her.
- God's cause for your life is easier to fulfill than your self-designed cause.
- When you find it, your true cause will liberate your passion and gifts.
- God's cause for you relates to helping and serving people.
- The best time to figure out the cause within you is now.

CHAPTER 5

DISCOVERING THE CAUSE OF A LIFETIME

ALFRED LOMAS, a forty-something man with dark, deep-set eyes and tattoo-covered neck and arms, looks like a veteran of the streets.

In fact, from the time he was a teenager, Alfred was involved with gangs. His life took a detour when he joined the Marines and became part of an elite team that trained with Special Forces units around the world. After his release, Alfred returned to Los Angeles and resumed his relationship with one of the major gangs. Given his military training and expertise, he was not only involved in a lot of violence but also in countersurveillance against the FBI, using many of the techniques he had learned overseas in covert ops. He worked directly for the relatively few gang leaders who were responsible for the majority of the violence that raged in the streets. He was responsible for protecting gang leaders, prostitution rings, drug sales, and the like.

A major gang war broke out involving the Crips, the original street gang that now operates all over the world. Alfred was right in the middle of all of this. Not long ago he told me that the two-and-a-half-square-mile area in downtown Los Angeles where that war raged had the highest murder rate in the country at that time. Alfred was the person responsible for introducing methamphetamines to the area, and he even got hooked on them. His life was a disaster. Eventually he wound up in jail.

His case involved acts of police corruption, so it was thrown out of court. But with most of his cohorts still sitting in jail, either awaiting their trial or serving time, he had nobody to turn to. There were riots happening in the jail, so it was in lockdown, preventing him from making the contacts he needed to get access to money just to survive. Because it was such a volatile time, the other people he knew who might have helped him had gone underground, leaving him broke and without the connections he needed.

Out of desperation, Alfred accepted an invitation to come to the Dream Center. He came hoping to get several hot meals and a few nights of decent rest. He ended up staying for a year.

During his time at the center, Alfred did more than break off his ties with his gang. He discovered the cause that restored dignity and meaning to his life. Today Alfred is involved in our food truck ministry, which distributes food to poor people. We hand out about one million pounds of food each month, for free, to poor people all over Los Angeles and to other churches who distribute it to people in their area. During the past three years or so, Alfred has been on the truck that serves people in the area he has lived and worked in all his life, the portion of the city where his gang and rival gangs terrorized people. While serving there, God impressed upon him the need to reach back into the gangs and get those people out of that life.

Alfred came to the Dream Center just hoping to survive. Most people back then would have put the odds of his rebuilding his life—let alone helping formulate a solution to Los Angeles's gang problem—as very low. And yet he has.

By now I hope you realize that, just as certainly as God put a cause inside of Alfred, He has one for you. Let's start at the beginning of the process. Once you realize that God has a cause just for you, how do you figure out what it is?

Having listened to a lot of people talk about their struggle to identify the cause within them, I need to assert one particular truth: *God wants you to know your cause.* He does not play games. Because He loves you more than you can understand, He is not going to make the discovery of your cause a tug-of-war in which He simply messes with your head. He designed that cause specifically for you because He knows it will deliver tremendous joy and fulfillment. When you figure it out and commit to it, a win-times-four situation emerges: your life takes on its ultimate meaning, the people you serve are blessed, the world becomes a better place, and God takes pleasure in your obedience and enjoyment.

So how do you find out what your cause is? From experience—mine and others'—I'd argue that the first step is to surrender your will to God. Not surprisingly, that step came fairly easy to Alfred, since he was already at the end of himself. But it's just as critical for you and me. I know surrender is not a popular idea in an age of independence and self-absorption, but the cornerstone of releasing the power of the cause within you is to affirm in your own mind, heart, and spirit that God knows what is best for you and that you are willing to do what He has ordained for you. If you know much about God, you recognize that He has your best interests in mind; any cause that He prepares for you will be something that produces good outcomes in every dimension. It is an application of the biblical passage that reminds us, "If God is for us, who can ever be against us?"[7]

One common mistake people make is to decide what they think

the cause should be, develop a plan, and then ask God to bless their plan. That's exactly what I did when I came to Los Angeles. I was determined that I was going to build a great church for God, and I had an entire plan in mind of just how to do it. My prayer was not that God would reveal His perfect cause for me but that He would bless my earnest plans for Him. The results of that gambit proved just how backward my approach was. While I suspect God appreciates our effort to do something great for Him, only He knows what is best for us and for His Kingdom. So rather than starting with self

While I suspect God appreciates our effort to do something great for Him, only He knows what is best for us and for His Kingdom.

and working out a plan that you want Him to accept, seek whatever He has in mind for you and adopt His plan. He says we should seek first the things of His Kingdom and everything else will fall into place,[8] and this is a perfect situation through which you can prove the viability of that notion.

The importance of this perspective cannot be overestimated. One of its many benefits is that it helps us distinguish between God's speaking to us and our convincing ourselves of something. Some psychologists describe that latter voice as "self-talk"—the running conversations we have with ourselves throughout each day as we try to use logic to make sense of reality and respond intelligently. If you are open to surrendering your will to God and accepting His direction and objectives for your life by faith, the nature of your self-talk will shift to being words that affirm His direction and probe the possibilities for carrying out the cause He has placed within you.

On a practical level, you may be wondering how God will "speak" to you. Most people never hear an audible voice telling them what to do. Yet He communicates clearly and unmistakably with each of us if we know what to be attentive to and how to respond.

In my life, God speaks through passion and circumstances. In other words, He instills a sense of desire and urgency within me. I have a passion to accomplish certain dreams. Because those dreams are not the normal human impulses, especially in today's self-indulgent culture, I believe those are God-inspired passions.

He further speaks to me by facilitating action related to that passion. He does that by placing me in circumstances that arouse my desire to respond. For instance, a number of times I have been driving around the neighborhood and seen something that needs attention. Suddenly, my adrenaline level shoots sky-high. One time I saw some kids playing basketball in the street without a court or a hoop; they were just throwing the ball in a garbage can they had elevated on a chair. Immediately I thought, *Note to self: provide a regulation basketball court in a safe place with real backboards and hoops for neighborhood kids*. I could have driven by without noticing the kids, absorbed in my thoughts, or I could have seen them and thought, *Oh, that's creative, good for them*, or, *Why don't those kids walk a half mile to the nearest school, climb the chain-link fence, and play on the outdoor court there?* But God was opening my eyes and stirring my passion to respond to a need that He would help me address.

I received my breakthrough revelation from God at Echo Park only after obeying an instinct to do what that internal voice was telling me: *Get out of bed, go down to the park, and wait for Me*. From a cultural standpoint, following that instinct was irrational. It was the wrong time of day; it was the wrong place to go (i.e., dangerous); and God had not been answering my direct prayers, so why would He awaken me after midnight and require such an exercise? But that's how God works. I think it's one way He tests us to see how willing we are to do what He asks.

If I had not obeyed that instinct, I would not have understood the cause He embedded deep within me. I might still be crying into my pillow in my apartment today, grieving over my inability to grow a great church for God. That's why I needed to listen to Him. He wasn't interested in my plans to build Him a great church; He already knew they'd amount to nothing. He had the perfect future set up for me, but I had to be willing to discard my inadequate dream and instead embrace His.

Even though I have been trained as a preacher, I will admit that so often the Holy Spirit is mysterious and unpredictable to me. The Holy Spirit is God's vehicle through whom He speaks to us, but He rarely communicates in audible tones. More often, the Spirit operates as our spiritual conscience, directing us in ways that require us to be led rather than to lead.

Through the Holy Spirit, God may "speak" to you in different ways. Sometimes it is through the internal impressions you receive. Other times it might be an audible voice. Occasionally you might be impacted by circumstances that God uses to grab your attention or direct your energy. In other situations God might reveal His plan for you through what someone else says to you: sometimes the voice of God is disguised as that of other people.

Of course, we often don't even know He is speaking. Why not? Because we anticipate His response coming at a particular time or in a specific manner, and He fails to conform to our expectations. Other times He speaks, but we cannot hear His voice over the noise of our lives: we are so distracted, focused on other matters, that when He conveys His message, we miss it.

Are you trying to figure out your cause? Have you been frustrated because you believe God has not spoken to you? Maybe the obstacle is that you're not sensitive to His voice. Or like me, perhaps you have been so determined to do it your way that you could not accept the signs and situations He placed in your path to capture your attention and get you on the right track.

I am a big believer that there are no accidents in life and that God wastes no human experience—only we do. In other words, when we experience pain or hardship, we do our best to overcome it and put distance between ourselves and that difficulty. Yet those downtimes might be exactly the springboard that God will use to propel you into the cause that will change your life and many others. *Your cause may be related to the pain and suffering you have endured.* Often your cause is revealed when you are at the lowest point of the valley, not on the pinnacle of the mountain.

Alfred Lomas is a great example of how God works in this way. Though Alfred seemed to have caught a break when his case was thrown out of court and he was released from prison, he returned to his old neighborhood with no idea of how to escape his past. So Alfred began wandering around the streets, trying to figure out what to do. And then God met him. An elderly woman from Canada who was visiting the Dream Center for a week as part of a church mission trip saw Alfred and walked right up to him. Alfred's recollection of that experience is priceless:

Often your cause is revealed when you are at the lowest point of the valley, not on the pinnacle of the mountain.

> I'm walking down the street and I see this grandmother. She sees me and immediately heads over to me. She had the most brilliant smile in the world; there was something about her smile that was just so dazzling. Keep in mind, I'm fresh out of jail, I'm still part of the gang world, and most of the people who saw me on the street or even in jail just turned around and walked the other way. I was hard and mean. You didn't want to have anything to do with me. But here comes this grandmother, smiling her bright smile, and she just

walks right up to me, bold in love, and asks, "Hi, how're you doing? Have you heard of the Dream Center?"

My first thought was, *This old lady must be crazy—there's something wrong with her.* And I looked behind her, and there's this pack of jokers coming up behind her, but they, too, had this beautiful aura of love and a giving spirit. I could sense it.

But immediately I felt these walls going up inside of me. You see, when I was really young, I was exposed to a very legalistic, highly condemning group that called itself "Christian." So that built in me a hatred for Christians. I mean I literally hated Christians and Christianity and anything to do with authority. When I was working in the gang and protecting a drug dealer, I was around people who took the drugs a lot. Sometimes I'd hear them cry out to God. They'd be wailing about how they were getting divorced, or their money had run out, or they were on a drinking binge and really messed up—all these hard-luck situations. But once they started praying to God, a fury welled up inside of me. I'd pistol-whip them, or hit them, or throw them out because they were praying. Then I'd ask them, "Where's your God now?" The hypocrisy I'd experienced as a kid really boiled inside of me, and I just hated Christians and churches.

So here's this eighty-year-old lady smiling sweetly in my face, and I was about to cuss her out and tell her what to do with her church and her God—but I just couldn't do it. I was fascinated by this old woman and her love and the fact that she didn't know or care who I was, she just loved me. And she asked me again if I'd heard of the Dream Center. I'd been in LA most of my life, but I pretty much stuck to my streets, so I'd never heard of it. But I remember thinking,

That's kind of a strange name. She moved a step closer to me, and I remember looking in these beautiful blue eyes she had—they just reflected love—and then she took my hand and very gently said, "If you need a place to stay, we have a place for you."

I was just drawn to that spirit that was working through her. Then a miracle happened. I asked her, "Really? What kind of place do you have?" I mean, that was not like me. I heard myself saying those words; it was like an out-of-body experience. I was thinking, *What are you doing, man?* I heard my voice, but it just couldn't have been me speaking. But it was.

So she called over the guy from the Dream Center who was in the pack of jokers behind her, and he explained that they have a one-year program. And I'm thinking that I only need a day or two to make my connections and get back to my life, but even if they have barbed wire and fences and video cameras, I can break through that stuff. So I told them, sure, I'd sign up for the one year.

We started walking toward the Dream Center, and I asked the lady where it was. She was from Canada and had no idea where we were or where the center was from there, but she looked up in the hills and saw the Hollywood sign, and she said, "It's in Hollywood." And right away I froze up a bit and thought, *Oh no, it's a cult.* So we kept walking and I started to wonder what the catch was. We walked over to a bus that would take us to the Dream Center, I got on it, and all these people were on it singing songs to Jesus, and I was thinking, *Oh Lord, this is the Charles Manson family. I'd better be on guard; there's something weird going on here.* That stuff was all totally foreign to me.

The bus finally started up, and we're driving someplace—

to the Dream Center, I hoped—and these people were all happy and singing. I sat there looking at them and still wondering, *What's the catch?* We got to the Dream Center and—well, here I am, six years later, still working with them, a transformed person. The catch was unconditional love. I went through the discipleship program. One day turned into a week. One week became a month. Three months into it I gave my life to the Lord. It was not because of what these people said to me but because of what I saw and experienced—people's passion for loving others. There was something profound about that, and with my background it had a really deep impact on me. You never know the power of servanthood and exactly how God works in a person's life.

As you know, Alfred volunteered to get involved in the food truck ministry and to help disciple other young men off the streets. Recently he also started an organization called LA Gang Tours. It provides an opportunity for people to tour the gang area, meet some of the gangsters, and better understand that life. His dream is that people will understand how gangs operate and will bring viable solutions and alternatives to gang-vulnerable areas, as well as to the gang members themselves. He also wants to help break the multigenerational bondage of gang membership. The money he makes from the tours goes into efforts to create jobs and business options in South Central Los Angeles, as a practical way of getting people out of the gang world. Because of his relationships and credibility with all the gangs, he has negotiated a peace treaty with them—times when there is an agreed-upon cease-fire and he can conduct his tours. He is also using his connections to begin working on ways to address the growth of the Mexico-based gangs that have branched out from LA.

One of the insights to draw from Alfred's journey is that his cause is a response to the pain and disappointment he experienced in his gang life. He is taking that bad experience and turning it into something positive. That's critical. Your pain can become the greatest motivation to embrace your cause. Does your pain crush you, or do you let it mold you and motivate you for positive results? Do you let your suffering overwhelm you and undermine your life, or do you use it as a means for growth?

Of course, not everybody has a story as dramatic as Alfred's—nor would I wish that upon people! Often the best way to figure out the cause within you is through the oldest method in the world: trial and error. In other words, if you're trying to figure out what God created you to do, just roll up your sleeves and start serving in cooperation with somebody else's cause. I cannot tell you how many times I encounter people who are clueless about their cause, but once they get involved in serving people—regardless of the nature of the service—God gives them situations or opportunities that instantly ring their bell.

I don't have to go any further than my wife to know how this process works. Caroline came to the Dream Center after finishing high school. Her father had taken a tour of our ministry, and knowing that she was searching for a way to serve people and grow in her faith, he suggested she check us out. She came, loved what she saw, and immediately signed up to spend a year with us as a volunteer. She didn't care what she was asked to do; she liked the vibe of the place and wanted to be on the streets, helping people.

If you're trying to figure out what God created you to do, just roll up your sleeves and start serving in cooperation with somebody else's cause.

When Caroline first started with us, the Dream Center was pretty new; things were not as developed or extensive as they are today. In the early days it was pretty common for everyone to fill a lot of different functions, including doing administrative work in the main office. Here is her recollection of what happened next:

One day I was answering phones at the reception desk. We got a call from a social worker who said there was a family in need of food and they only lived a couple of blocks away. So I loaded up my old '78 Volvo station wagon and headed over to the house. When I walked into that apartment, it changed my life forever. The woman was a single mom, twenty-five years old, and she had eight young kids, all by different fathers. Most of the kids were just in their underwear or diapers. She lived with all those children in a little apartment with no furniture and just a couple of couch cushions on the floor. The moment we walked in the door with these bags of food, the kids jumped in our arms and started eating raw zucchini. Now how hungry are children when they jump in a stranger's arms and start eating raw zucchini?

So when I saw what the life of a hungry child looked like here in LA, I knew I couldn't just go back to the office and keep answering phones; I had to do something about it. We always had a food bank here, but what I discovered is that many people who really need the food don't even have a way to get here to pick it up. They don't have transportation, and they can't just leave their kids at home.

And that's when we got the idea for the food trucks. I saw an old truck sitting in the parking lot and asked the pastor if we could use it to deliver food to people. He said sure. I picked out a few elementary schools in nearby neighborhoods. We pulled up right when school was letting out, which gave us an automatic crowd, and went up to the ladies who had walked there to get their children. All the moms had little helpers to help them carry the food home. So all of a sudden the food truck ministry was up and running.

Even though Caroline didn't feel that was really her cause, she wanted to help people, and when she found a need, she dealt with it. She was great at it, too, helping to build the food truck outreach into one of our cornerstone efforts. But though she enjoyed it and saw tremendous results from her efforts—it was satisfying in that sense—the food truck wasn't her passion.

The funny thing about her involvement with that activity is that I totally misread the situation. I met Caroline while she was a volunteer at the Dream Center, running the food truck ministry, and eventually we got married. For several years I watched her serve people from the food trucks and thought how wonderful it was that God brought me a wife whose primary cause was to support me as I pursued my cause. But He was about to teach me something important. Here's what Caroline says:

> During my first seven years at the Dream Center, I was out on the streets five or six days a week, serving food and ministering to people. One day I was talking to a friend of mine who was very passionate about orphans and kids in foster care, who are part of many of the families we feed. She told me some statistics about the situation. The one that stood out to me was that more than half of the kids in foster care have parents who love them but lose those kids due to the lack of basic necessities. Those moms love their kids. They're doing all they can to get by, but they lose their children because they don't have enough food or other basic necessities, like a refrigerator or beds.
>
> So I thought about that and what it must be like for those

women. Social workers give these families a list of things the family has to comply with before the social worker returns at a prescribed time for an inspection. If you've done your best to satisfy everything on the list but you haven't quite accomplished or acquired everything mandated, then you know that when the inspection comes, they're going to remove your children. That's how the system works. I couldn't even imagine what the prayers of those mothers must be like.

I wondered what these families would think about a church and about God if they stepped in and saved the family from losing their kids? So I asked Matthew if it would be okay for me to start an outreach to those moms. He was enthusiastic about it, so we started it up, and it has been going for about a year now. Last year we saved two hundred families from being split apart and we've reunified another fifty families that were split apart.

We have developed a good working relationship with the Department of Child and Family Services. They know we want to keep the families together. They will refer families who are on the edge to us, so we get calls every single day asking us to help those families get what they need so they can meet the department's requirements and stay together. We stay in close contact with those families, visiting them every week to make sure they are doing okay. And we are excited that many of those families—more than 80 percent of them—also get connected to the church.

When we start working with a family, we also test the education level of the parents. We can then help them pursue their dream, using their gifts and abilities, so they're not always just trying to survive. We want them to thrive. For example, Mary was one of the moms we helped out. She was in her forties, had four children, and she couldn't read.

When we evaluated her, she tested at a first-grade level. Can you imagine that? We found out that she had been molested by her father when she was eight, wound up in foster care, and lived in forty different homes by the time she reached eighteen. When she was emancipated at eighteen, she had no education, no job skills—nothing that enabled her to deal with life successfully. I still don't know how she got by all these years.

Mary has been going through our tutoring program. She's the oldest person in her class. She gets embarrassed about it and really struggles to keep up. She's up to a third-grade level now, and doing well, but it's really difficult for older people. We work with all kinds of volunteers who come to us saying they want to see God do a miracle, but the miracle for Mary would be somebody willing to commit to teaching her how to read and write. That would change her life, the lives of her children, and the lives of future generations coming from her family.

You know, all of this came to a head for me a couple of years ago, after I watched a program called *Invisible Children*, about children who are left behind in this world. It all seemed so unjust. I asked God in my prayers why it was happening and felt His response was that He'd already paid the price and guaranteed the resources, so the real question was why *I* was allowing it to happen. That really changed my view of this kind of work. But honestly, I had no idea how passionate I was about these things until I got out there and started working with the people. I am happiest when I am out on the streets helping people. And it's so ironic that the things that break my heart are the same things that can bring me such pleasure. Being used by God as part of the solution is incredibly satisfying.

> When you step into your cause, the good news is that God wants it done even more than you do. He'll do whatever is necessary to make it work. If you just show up and do what you can, He makes you look like a genius!

Like many pastors, I had fallen into the trap of thinking that my wife's cause was to help me. I used to wonder why so many pastors' wives were so miserable. Wasn't supporting their husband in his pastorate enough? So many of those women feel resigned to watching their husband do his thing without having a chance to pursue their own calling and passions. Thanks to Caroline, it finally dawned on me that there is a big difference between being happy and being fulfilled. She was happy serving people, doing things that fit my ministry vision and staying within the confines of the service opportunities we had in place, but it did not truly fulfill her. I had never asked what her driving passion or her great cause was. How insensitive of me! Thankfully, she found her cause and is changing the world through it.

Over time I've worked with a lot of people who had no clear understanding of their unique cause but were willing to get involved and try out different things. To figure out the great cause within you, you don't have to have your life totally together, or have figured out the details of your future or even the nature of the cause. You start by substituting God's will for yours; then you test drive the practice of serving people and let God orchestrate everything from there.

You might discover your cause by simply becoming aware of other people's needs. Since your cause is all about alleviating human need of one type or another, stay alert to the needs you witness and how those spark your imagination and passion. Chances are you will be introduced to your cause through such exposure.

Caroline's work with families fell into place because while she was serving people with one set of needs, she was able to observe the broader spectrum of their lives and needs. In the midst of that, she also had opportunities to speak with other servants who offered their perceptions and ideas. It was out of those observations and conversations that she came in contact with a need that touched her heart at a very deep level.

Like most people, once Caroline encountered that cause, she knew it was her special focus. It hasn't stopped her from helping people in a variety of ways and situations, but her primary focus is working with those families on the edge of being torn apart for lack of tangible goods that we can supply. Other ways of helping people have grown out of that. For instance, Mary's experience inspired us to start a related program, the Emancipation Home, to take in teenagers who are turned out of the foster care system but are not ready to take care of themselves. It's a lot easier to help people when they're young than later on in life. This ministry, too, began with Caroline tuning in to what she was seeing, hearing, and sensing as she helped people.

About ten years ago, Kelli Bradley visited the Dream Center for a short-term mission trip with a college group the week after she graduated. She returned home to Arkansas, but a couple of months later she came back to the Dream Center to volunteer for a year. Originally she felt called to serve Caroline and me. For years she worked faithfully at all kinds of tasks, learning everything we do at the Dream Center.

Through her experience of working with several pregnant teenagers who were struggling to get by, she discovered that her passion was working with hurting families. When my wife started working with foster-care families, she asked Kelli to join her. It was a great match. They were terrific partners for a couple of years, getting that project off the ground. Then Kelli helped increase the number of foster parents and adoptive parents. We wound up renting homes for foster parents to begin taking in children who desperately needed a family.

That evolved into Kelli helping us provide housing and services for homeless families that have lost their income and housing and need transitional assistance to get back on their feet. She now oversees more than two dozen families living at the Dream Center, allowing the families to stay together through their toughest times. That's usually when such families break apart from the stress and financial hardships. While they're at the center, we help them find their dream and prepare to pursue it. But Kelli found out her passion for these things by spending time serving Caroline and me, experiencing different types of service, and feeling her heart particularly moved when working with those kinds of families.

If you're serious about knowing God's chosen cause for you, think carefully before you turn down invitations to help somebody you know engage in some type of service activity, no matter how big or small it might be. That invitation might be the beginning of the adventure that identifies the means to filling the hole in your heart.

Kelli also points out that the baggage from their pasts keeps many people from being able to move forward toward their as-yet-unidentified dream. Maybe you or someone close to you has gone through times so difficult that it prevents progress. We've found that those hurts and fears must be addressed in order to deal with the pain. Whether that is through counseling or other forms of assistance, dreaming about how to make the most of your life and how to make the world a better place is more likely to happen once you are freed from the bondage of painful memories or practices. Healing facilitates helping just as helping promotes healing.

Once people get past that garbage from the past, they are ready to stop focusing on themselves and think creatively and freely about the future and how to contribute value. It's pretty common for us to see people who have been stuck on their problems suddenly light up once they get past those issues and become excited about what they can do. Everyone has strengths and interests that point the way to their causes. Being sufficiently liberated from your pain or limitations to experiment with your strengths and passion—without having to struggle with survival or personal anguish—is a major step toward honoring God through your cause. Kelli frequently reminds people that it's easier to help people than you might think, but sometimes you have to help yourself get to a place where you can bless others with your best thinking and effort.

When you're in the process of trying to figure out your cause, here's one last piece of advice: *your breakthrough may happen when you least expect it.* The provision and identification of your cause is a gift from God to you; it's not in your power to control when you discover the cause. You may do whatever you can to be ready to receive that understanding, but you cannot force the timing. When God is ready to reveal the cause, He'll do so. My observation is that He often seems to do so when you're truly ready to embrace the cause.

My Echo Park experience underscores this principle. Until I was so brokenhearted that I didn't know what else I could possibly do, I was not really prepared to listen. After all, I thought I had already figured out what God needed; I was going to build Him a great church. Had God revealed the cause to me before our encounter in Echo Park, it would have been a waste of time. Come to think of it, maybe He did try to reveal it prior to the encounter. I don't know; if He did, I certainly wasn't ready to listen because I was too focused on pursuing the cause of my making. It wasn't until I was out of energy, ideas, and hope that He had my attention. At that point He enlightened me.

That's probably the same course of action He'll take with you, too. The decision to finally surrender your will and your choice of cause is crucial to facilitating His revealing the cause to you.

Not sure what your cause is? Don't sit around doing nothing, waiting for the perfect circumstances to bring clarity. Not many of us jump from doing nothing into the ideal conditions for serving without some false starts, missteps, and hardships in between. Find some people you trust and would like to serve alongside of and get involved. While you're helping them, you'll be making a positive contribution to society, getting to know yourself better (your passions and strengths), and giving God more opportunities to speak to you about your cause. It's kind of like the Nike campaign: just do it!

WHAT I'VE LEARNED

- God wants you to know the cause He has for you, so ask Him to reveal it.
- Your cause relates to the needs of other people.
- Sometimes your cause emerges out of your pain or hardships.
- Serving alongside others often allows your passion to become clear.
- A breakthrough in identifying your cause may come when you least expect it.
- The first step is to surrender your will to His.

CHAPTER 6

LET NOTHING STAND IN YOUR WAY

ONE OF THE MORE COLORFUL CHARACTERS around the Dream Center is a guy named Barry. We met him during our Under the Bridge visits. After losing a good job as a civil engineer, he lived for seventeen years on the streets, the last ten of those sleeping under bridge overpasses. He'd stomp up to our campus three times a day for meals, then return to his place under the bridge. Finally, through frequent conversations with some of our people, he was saved and then enrolled in our discipleship program for recovering drug addicts. Now, five years later, he is not only sober, but he just finished Bible college! At the age of sixty, after wasting much of his life and health on drugs—he admits to being a heroin addict for eighteen years before moving to methamphetamines for another twenty—he is serving as the director of our chapel.

If you had talked to Barry six or seven years ago, he would have told you he would never again accomplish anything productive. But once he got sober and began taking care of himself, God gave him a dream. The dream included getting a theological education—even at his advanced age—and then using it to help other downtrodden people pick themselves up and move forward. This is how Barry explains how his life has changed:

> For years I ran from what my calling was, kind of like Jonah. I'm a good runner. I did all kinds of things these past few years, but I wasn't listening to the call. Finally, I was placed in charge of the chapel. And that's what all my education and preparation has been for. So now I'm consumed by it. We do eighteen chapel services each week, and it's wonderful. I understand these people because I was one of them for so long. After I got discharged from the military, I used the benefits to go to school. I have a lot of education, but I didn't have much smarts, if you know what I mean. Now I know that I will have a ministry to people on the streets, and I am so excited about that. There are so many good people on the streets, people in bad situations just trying to survive. God rescued me so I can help rescue them.

As surely as I know that Barry is guided by a God-given cause, I know that God has a cause that's just right for you. He has loaded it within your heart the same way that operating software is loaded on a computer's hard drive when you buy it. But in the same way that you might not know how to operate that software without further exploration and experimentation, you might not figure out your cause until you push through some obstacles that pop up. God isn't hiding the cause from you, but the cumulative effect of choices can blind you from seeing it or prevent you from being ready to accept it.

Among the obstacles you'll face are the countless distractions in your life. You're busy with all kinds of activities, commitments, responsibilities, and opportunities. Most of those endeavors revolve around taking care of yourself; responding to the needs of others may not even register on your radar. Another obstacle could be your priorities. We invest our resources in the things we deem most important and necessary, which range from addressing basic needs to experiencing consistent comfort and pleasure. Considerations regarding our cause get squeezed out of the picture.

Never confuse activity for significance and impact. Can we agree that meaning doesn't come from what we have to do to survive but from what we do that adds value to the lives of others? In other words, there are things you have to do to survive—earn a living, pay your bills, stay healthy, maintain relationships—but the acts that push you beyond survival and provide you with a greater sense of joy are those that make the world a better place. That means you have to make your cause every bit as important and central in your life as performing well in your vocation, eating healthy foods, and making sure your children are appropriately educated.

Never confuse activity for significance and impact.

My experience has been that people always hit snags along the way to living out their cause. Meeting other priorities is just one of them. Here are some others I've seen emerge that you should be aware of—and ready to overcome.

Some people refuse to do anything until they understand their options in full. Finding and fulfilling your cause doesn't work that way. God seems to provide what is known as *progressive revelation*: He shows you as much as you need to know (or can handle) and then unveils additional insight when it becomes appropriate. That makes sense:

if He showed you the scope of what He wants to do with you in the pursuit of your cause, it would blow your mind and scare you out of the process. Instead, He does what every great coach does: gives you just enough opportunity and responsibility to build yourself up so that you're ready to take the next step in your development.

Jesus modeled this approach when He began calling the apostles. He did not tell Peter, James, John, and the rest of the Twelve that He was taking them from their fishing routes and other simple jobs to build the Christian church that would change the course of human history. He did not explain that He was preparing them to scatter to different locations on the continent in order to challenge powerful and hostile rulers and to motivate people to live completely different lives. Had He done so, how many of the Twelve would have signed up for the ride? Probably none of them. Instead, He partnered with them to get them ready to fulfill their cause, giving them increasingly challenging tasks en route to becoming the first human leaders of the Christian church.

God wants you to succeed, so He's willing to take things one step at a time. But He also knows that the progressive development of your cause allows you to demonstrate and strengthen your commitment. After all, one of His guiding principles is that you have to prove yourself to be faithful with what you have been given before you are offered more opportunities.[9]

There is a lot I don't understand about life. But one thing I do know is that if God had told this twenty-year-old kid from the suburbs of Phoenix that within a few years he'd be in charge of a huge campus, more than two hundred outreach programs, a staff of several hundred people, an annual multimillion-dollar budget, and a building campaign of several million more, that young man would have totally freaked out. It would have been too much, too soon. In fact, if I didn't freak out over the scope of the vision, it would have been due to having an overgrown ego—and that arrogance and overconfidence would have made a total mess of the tremendous opportunities that were in store for the Dream Center.

Instead, God worked with me and moved me forward at just the right pace. It wasn't the pace everyone else thought was right: some said we were moving too slow; some said it was too fast. But God knows me better than I know myself, and He orchestrated the process perfectly. As long as I was willing to listen to Him and be obedient, everything would work out great. And it has. I have certainly made mistakes along the way—sometimes moving before God, sometimes not trusting Him enough and suffering because I waited too long. But overall it has been a wonderful experience of allowing God to build the church while I focus on helping to restore the lives of broken people.

God's dreams for you are always bigger—and better—than your dreams for you. He understands the appropriate and most beneficial time to open your eyes to those dreams as well.

So if you do not understand all the details or if you believe that the vision must be bigger than you currently understand it to be, don't let that stop you from beginning to act on what you know. Take whatever aspects of the cause God is willing to reveal to you now and run with them. He'll fill in the blanks when He is ready to do so—which usually means when you are capable of handling them.

> **God's dreams for you are always bigger— and better—than your dreams for you.**

While some people refuse to act if they don't have all the details, many other people stall in their drive to pursue their cause because even the limited vision God reveals overwhelms them. This happens because we underestimate the power of God working through us to accomplish His will. What's at issue is what I think of as the *miracle space*: the gap between what we can accomplish on our own and what can be accomplished when we allow God to work through us. In a culture that acts based on the tangible, we are reluctant to step out in faith and believe that God will fill in that gap. Perhaps if we prayed more often and more fervently for God to give us His power to take on the vision, we'd be more aggressive.

Jesus had some experience with this too. Think about the crippled man who had been sitting by the side of the pool in Bethesda (as described in John 5). Every day for almost four decades that man had been dependent on others to help him—some 13,870 days of powerless, agonized living. When Jesus walked through that court-yard, the man lay there passively. Then Jesus gave him a completely different response than anyone else had: pick up your bed and walk home. Jesus was asking the crippled man to do more than the man believed he was able to do. But when God is working with you, that miracle space makes all the difference—the gap is bridged between "I can't" and "I can!"

The existence of the Dream Center is a living testimony to the importance of trusting God to master that miracle space. When I was growing up, one day I asked my father, "Dad, is it possible for a church to be open twenty-four hours a day?" My father was always great about not wanting to squash my dreams. He was aware that the crazy questions I often asked might be a thought or dream that God had planted in me that needed to be cultivated. So he very wisely said, "I don't know, Matthew. Why don't you go ahead and build one someday?"

And, of course, it turns out that a 24-7 church *was* one of those God-implanted ideas. Thanks to the encouragement of my father and many others—and, of course, the blessing of God—that's exactly what the Dream Center has become. It has not happened because of my world-class leadership or my visionary planning. It happened because it was God's cause, and I was willing to let Him implement it through me. Building a 24-7 church is more than I can handle. It exists today only because God filled in that miracle space between the church I could initiate and manage through my natural talents and energy and the church that God had in mind.

We might never have gotten the church off the ground, though, if I had simply listened to the advice of people who make decisions without God. When we were establishing the church, many Christians pleaded with me not to establish the church in this area. One person was willing to fund the church if we went to Orange County; he was ready to write out a million-dollar check to get us started if we would locate the ministry there. My dad and I explained that we were called to Los Angeles, and we tried to encourage him to help us with that work, but the man insisted that he wouldn't give us a dime if we stayed in downtown LA because he would not fund a failure. Other Christians kept warning me that staying in the Echo Park area was a disaster in the making. They rightly pointed out that at best we'd be helping people who didn't have the resources to help us. "You can't build a great church there," they said. And they were right. I can't. But God can. He chose to. And He chose to use me to do it. It is the insane cause He sowed in my heart, the vision that keeps me excited and motivated, the miracle that He performs every day in downtown LA.

One of the most moving examples of someone grasping her cause and trusting God to handle more than she could possibly manage without Him is Alena Strickland. Shortly after her birth, Alena's daughter Jamie contracted an infection in her brain that required multiple surgeries. While she and her daughter stayed in the hospital, Alena found out about another infant who had been left at the hospital by her parents. This baby weighed less than a pound at birth and was given only a small chance of survival. She did not have healthy intestines, so she needed to be on a constant IV in order to get sufficient nutrition to fight for her life. Alena's daughter and this other child were about the same age, so they shared a hospital room for about eighteen months, at which point the doctor said the other child was not going to make it. Alena recalls that time with crystal clarity:

> At that point, I heard God telling me, "Take her home and let her die at your house." That little girl was black. At the time, I lived in a very white area, and during those years there was a lot of racial stuff going on. On top of that, I had a very sick daughter of my own plus two other small children at home and a husband who was not very supportive of this. Then I thought about the fact that I didn't know how to do black kids' hair, her teeth were really messed up from being on a pacifier all the time, I had no idea how to provide the medical care she'd need, we didn't have the machines she required, and things like that. And yet God kept saying, "Take her home, take her home."
>
> For weeks I wrestled with God, and I gave Him all my excuses and fears. It got to the point where I couldn't sleep. God just kept putting it in my head and my heart, every second of every day: "Take her home. Take her home. Take her home." Finally I did something I had never done before. I said, "Okay, God, this is it. I feel like You're telling me to do this. I'm telling You, You've got the wrong person. You're going to have to either audibly tell me, or You're going to have to show me something so there's no more doubt in my head." At that point I actually had two of my kids in the hospital, one of them in a crib and the other in a bed. I felt I was already in over my head.
>
> I threw the Bible down on the bed and told Him to show me. When I picked up my Bible, it fell open to James 1, and I started reading the chapter. I was thinking, *What a relief, this has nothing to do with anything. I'm clear on this one.* But then, of course, I got to the end of the chapter, down

to verse 27, where it says, "pure and genuine religion in the sight of God the Father means caring for orphans and widows in their distress." At that point, I just said, "Okay, God, this is it. I understand now."

So that day I went to the hospital people and asked them to start training me on how to care for her. Soon after that, we had her home with us for about a month before she died. I had learned all the medical care and all the machines. The hospital, of course, had my phone number, and after that they just started calling me to take care of more terminally ill kids.

And it became clear that I was called to that cause. God met me at every step of the journey. Every issue I had argued about with Him was no longer an issue. It just worked out. So I started taking the kids until my own children got a little bit older and it was getting to be too much for them to handle. At that point I told God it was over, but He said, "Nope, now I've got some kids that aren't going to die. They just have medical issues, and you know how to handle it."

That began in 1985. Today, after twenty-five years of caring for the people God has called her to love, Alena and her family have taken in and served 170 suffering children. That number includes fifteen who have become permanent parts of her family through adoption or guardianship. At every point along the way, God has given her the knowledge, patience, resources, and whatever else she has needed to make it work. She often speaks to other people about her journey and encourages them to believe that the cause God gives them is one He will help them master:

I know some people are amazed at what I do, but it has become no big deal at all. It's not even a hard thing to do anymore; it's just what I do.

I encourage others to step up and do whatever God calls them to. You can do it. After all, I've been able to do something that is certainly beyond what I know how to do, and I have had no special training or preparation—nothing at all, really. My husband left me while my daughter was in a series of comas and the doctors were telling us that she wasn't going to live much longer. He just couldn't take it, along with the other children we were caring for. He met me at home one day and said, "This is it. You either stop going to the hospital and staying with her or I'm leaving." I said, "Well, I can't leave her. I've got to be with our daughter in the hospital." I came home from the hospital later that day, and he was gone.

So I've done most of this while I was single. God met me at every point and has helped me handle each new disability and every new challenge. Whatever God calls you to do—it doesn't matter what it is—He will meet you there and give you what you need to do it.

I watch someone like Alena, who often partners with the Dream Center in ministering to families, and marvel at how God works through His chosen people—normal, ordinary people like her or you or me—to do these incredible things. Alena also tells people about all the other ways He has taken care of her needs. She remarried about ten years ago, and her husband helps her with all of the children. Their home—1,900 square feet, which is not big by Southern California standards, and certainly not large for a household that includes ten or more people, most of whom have special needs—has proven to be sufficient for what they do. She admits that her life is difficult socially and spiritually. She can't go out to lunch with her friends in the middle of the day: who could babysit for so many kids who have such special needs and who sometimes become physically violent? She and her husband don't get many social invitations either. Vacations are next to impossible. She also acknowledges that they don't get a lot of sleep.

The kicker was that after having attended a church for forty-five years, she was asked not to return because the presence of the children was too stressful for the congregation. And none of that bothers her:

> You know, that's just a small price to pay. I'm not complaining about any of that. Things happen, and people have different reactions, but I love what God has called me to do, and He has given me an eternal perspective on the short time I have on earth.
>
> Once you've had God call you to something that you're totally incapable of and yet you do it, you really learn to trust God a lot faster. I'm still learning how to fully trust Him. I have more to learn, but every day I have to give everything to God and be careful not to allow my own nature to take over. I know beyond a shadow of a doubt He called me to this, and I know He wouldn't leave me unable to do it. He has proven Himself over and over; it works.
>
> I think a lot of people listen for their cause and then they just say, "No, I can't do it." Just like I did. Literally, I told God, "You've got the wrong person. Physically, I can't do this." But I've learned that you need to be still and know that He's God and simply listen. If He says to do something really crazy, check it out. I wasted months going back and forth with Him before realizing He was right. Based on my experience, at least, I believe God will tell you what the calling is if you listen, and then He'll make a way for you if you're willing. I fought against it for a long time. It wasn't something I minded doing. I didn't think, *Oh, that's gross, drawing blood and doing those other things*. It wasn't that.

I felt I simply could not do what was required physically and I did not have the technical skills and capability.

On top of that, I wasn't sure about losing all my family members and friends. You've got to be willing to lose all that. But really, is it that big of a deal if you don't get to have your nails done, or your hair done, or go on that big vacation? Really, is it that big of a deal when you're giving eternity to people? You've got to be willing to basically lose everything, and then God gives it back to you when you answer His call and when you walk in His will. He gives it all back to you.

It would have been easy for Alena to fall back on her lack of expertise or experience as a good reason not to step out in faith and pursue her cause. Alena proves, however, that when God is in it with you, you can do more—a lot more—than you think you can do. There are all kinds of excuses you can come up with to avoid pursuing your cause, but in the end that will just leave you empty.

When David took on Goliath, he was accepting a challenge that everyone knew he could not accomplish. He embraced it because he felt called to the challenge and believed that God would support him.[10] I look at people like Alena and Barry and realize that they do not have the human capabilities to pull off what God has asked them to do. But they do it because of their obedience to the call and their trust in God's love for them. They do more than they can do. You can too.

Another obstacle to pursuing the cause may be the lack of resources we assume are needed to get the job done. In our desire to avoid failure, we do our best to imagine what it will take to complete the task we believe God has given us. We want to be good stewards of our finances and opportunities, so we halt everything until we have the resources in hand or at least lined up.

But you have to remember that fulfilling your cause is a matter of obedience and faith. You have to be wise, but you also have to be spiritually sensitive. Prayer is critical—not the kind through which you tell God what to do but the kind through which He tells you what He is up to. When God tells you to go, your current lack of resources is not a viable excuse not to go. He may simply be preparing an opportunity to fill in the miracle space.

If I had waited until we had the funds to do our different forms of outreach to hurting people, I doubt I'd be writing this book today. When we had the opportunity to save a girl from sexual trafficking, we had no program and no budget for that kind of service. It costs us more than $250,000 each year to help girls escape from trafficking and then help them get their life and their dream back. Yet we do it, believing God called us to it. He has faithfully provided the money.

> Prayer is critical—not the kind through which you tell God what to do but the kind through which He tells you what He is up to.

When we saw how the current recession is destroying so many families, we had no room or money to take in desperate families who wound up on the streets. We had no program to help them get back on their feet and focus on their dream. But we launched out in faith, and God has been providing the $150,000 that effort costs us each year. Money, space, and other tangible needs cannot be used as the barrier that prevents you from doing what God calls you to do. You may have to get creative, and everything may not be as proper and pristine as you'd prefer, but the most important thing is trusting God and responding to His call.

These are very tough times economically. The United States has millions of hurting people, millions of families that are on (or over) the edge, millions of young people who are making bad choices in life, millions of older people who are living in hardship because their savings have been wiped out. Churches and nonprofit organizations have been hit hard by the reduction in people's giving. There are plenty of good reasons not to take risks in the pursuit of your cause. But now is *not* the time for us to shrink back in fear and uncertainty. If we can't do what people need when they need it the most, then why are we here? What value do we bring to the world? This is a season of great need; it requires people of great faith who will invest in people's lives and dreams. It is the best time ever for you to influence the shape and well-being of the world.

If I had waited until I had everything in hand, there would be no Dream Center today. By the grace of God, I was encouraged to keep pushing the boundaries of the dream He gave me. So we started with a little church building and a couple of small homes down the street. As we pursued the cause, we filled up that space and the other houses that we rented. One day I was driving down the Route 101 freeway, about a mile and a half from Bethel Temple, and I looked to my left and saw this massive building, this 400,000-square-foot hospital, just sitting right there like a cargo ship docked against the freeway. It had a big For Sale banner on it. I'd never even noticed that massive building before. Immediately I thought, *That's it! That's the place for us. A hospital for broken people—it's the perfect fit.*

So I did some calling around and found out the story regarding that building. It was the old Queen of Angels Hospital owned by the Catholic church, and they were trying to sell the property. The building had been sitting vacant for a while, and it needed a lot of renovations. It had been on the market a while too. One of the major movie studios had put in a bid for the building, which was about to be accepted. The plan was to expand their movie studio to that location and make films there.

Immediately we got in touch with the people representing the property and talked to them about what we do and the possibility of buying the building. They told us the movie studio's bid was around $15 million. I told the hospital representatives outright, "We really don't have that kind of money, but we've got a dream." They were really stirred by the vision and told me to make them an offer. My dad and I had not expected the meeting to go that well, or for things to move so quickly, so we had not discussed strategy, pricing, and the rest. But it was our moment, and we knew we couldn't just walk away; if we did, we felt the opportunity would be lost. So we kind of threw out a wild number, just to see what would happen. We offered $3.9 million.

To our shock they said, "We love your vision. This is wonderful. We'll call the lawyers and agents to get the process started." Well, we didn't know what to say. It was too good to be true. Only God could orchestrate this sale when the owners already had an offer for nearly four times as much money from a more financially respectable organization. In a way, though, it didn't surprise me, because from the moment I first noticed the building and that huge For Sale banner waving in the breeze, I knew this was supposed to be our new home.

Of course, the downside was that we didn't have $3.9 million. In fact, we didn't even have $1 million.

The scope of this provision and its timing were unexpected, to say the least. After my Echo Park encounter with God, I was thrilled to have that little Bethel Temple property, and I just figured I'd be there forever. We were happy to be plodding away in that neighborhood, based at a tiny church that you couldn't find if you tried. During my first years there, various people who were scheduled to visit Bethel sometimes couldn't find it, even when they'd been sent maps and directions ahead of time.

Bethel Temple's difficult location wasn't our only challenge: by the grace of God, we had outgrown the facilities. That didn't seem like a big deal to me; I simply figured we'd be there forever and somehow make it work. You do what you can with what you have. I was at peace with that notion. God had delivered me to my cause, and this was clearly the place where I was meant to pursue that cause, so we'd figure out a way to buy or rent more homes in the immediate area in order to help more people. From a human perspective the Bethel property was inadequate to accomplish what needed to be done. But *none* of what was already happening made sense from a human perspective. Given that, we believed that God knew what He was doing. He'd placed us at Bethel, and we'd just keep doing what we were called to do and let Him worry about the rest.

So when the hospital option arose, it seemed like the opportunity of a lifetime. The money could have been an issue, but we didn't let it be. If God did not want us there, they would not have accepted the offer. If we misread the situation, we trusted that the deal would fall apart during the closing proceedings. But we fully expected everything to move forward.

The purchase of the hospital campus—a nine-acre campus that included eight other buildings and several parking lots as well as the fifteen-story hospital building—was God's continuing provision for a group of people who were sold out to His cause. All of a sudden, when God feels you're ready, He does a miracle. At some point He may say, "Okay, we're moving up to the big leagues now." That might happen as a result of your past faithfulness, or it might happen to boost your faith; I've seen it take place both ways. In our case, I believe we'd slogged our way through so many tests and pushed through so many ordinary days that buying the hospital was a result of God's seeing our commitment and willingness to continue in a hidden place with unwanted people, without adequate funding, media fanfare, or celebrity involvement. And what He has done through that building is to create an extraordinary cause on the foundation of a lot of little days and simple acts of love and kindness that largely went unnoticed except by those whose lives were altered by those efforts.

By the way, getting the money for the hospital purchase—and then millions more for renovations and upgrades—is another story we'll get to later. Suffice it to say I had no clue how to get my hands on $3.9 million, but God did, and we own the building free and clear today because we were willing to let God fill in that miracle space.

I know somebody who reads this is going to be thinking about people, including some ministers, who have "stepped out in faith" because "God spoke to them" only to wind up embarrassing God and the Christian body by defaulting on a loan or some other agreement, creating black-eye experiences for the Kingdom of God. Those situations do occur. But in my mind, you have to recognize the difference between stepping out in faith because you believe you are skilled enough to make it happen versus stepping out in faith based on the clear and consistent call of God and the knowledge that there is no way you can make it happen on your own. As always, the proof is in the results.

As you get ready to make a difference through your cause, rest assured that you will be criticized. Some people will be jealous. Others will be angry. Some will misunderstand your motives. Others are highly competitive and don't want anyone taking the spotlight from their own work. Some of your critics will be people who do work similar to yours; others will be people who are clueless about what you do. No matter where the negative words come from, just know they will come. And be ready to turn criticism to your advantage.

From a very early age I knew I would become a spiritual leader of some type. I expected my role to be that of a pastor. Given that, I worked on my preaching skills even as an adolescent and teenager.

Finally, when I was sixteen, I was given my first preaching opportunity. My dad is a terrific preacher, known throughout the world for his ability to communicate effectively; many people expected me to have the same gift.

I practiced my message for weeks, knowing that this could be my breakthrough moment. By the time the day arrived for me to preach, I had my content ready, had worked hard on delivery techniques, and was eager to take the stage. But I was so nervous that I finished my entire forty-five-minute presentation in five minutes. Five minutes! My dad had been telling me for years that I needed to slow down, pace myself, enunciate, and allow people's ears to catch up with my tongue. I wasn't able to follow his advice that day. I also had a stuttering problem, which was magnified by the speed of my delivery. Well, it all hit the fan that day.

As I was walking out of the church building after that humiliating experience, I passed by a conference room in which a couple of the older pastors were sitting. The door was partially open, so I was able to hear their conversation. One veteran pastor said to his colleague, without knowing I was within earshot, "His granddaddy and his daddy are fine preachers, but it's really sad to see a young man do what he's not called to do. And that boy is certainly not called to preach."

That crushed me. I took five steps toward the wall and just knocked my head against it, distraught at my failure. Who did I think I was fooling? Tears started falling to the carpet as I felt my hope of serving God slip away. I slinked out the nearest door in a total daze, crying the whole way to my grandmother's house. I was convinced I was the biggest failure in the world, and now the word was out.

After blindly walking two miles to her house, I flopped on a bed and continued to weep. My grandmother entered the room and asked how I was doing. "Grandma," I confided, "those preachers said I'm no good and I should never preach again." My grandma, who had been in the church and witnessed my dismal performance, said something that was so powerful. "I can't believe those men said that. You were amazing. You sounded like Billy Graham up there. You were incredible." That lifted my spirits enough to realize that all I needed to do was refuse to let a bad experience and harsh criticism negate my call to serve God. I used that criticism as a motivation to get better. I didn't like the nasty words spoken about me, but they fueled a determination to never again give those men reason to think that God had not called me to serve Him by preaching.

And I always say, thank God for lying grandmas!

That sure wasn't the last time my best efforts have been ripped apart by others:

- In the early years several pastors from other churches visited to tell me they knew I wouldn't stay at Bethel Temple once the church grew and I had a chance to leave for a more comfortable and prestigious suburban setting.
- Professionals have written and called to tell me that our recovery programs are worthless because they do not use the latest and greatest clinical techniques and rely too much on faith in Christ.
- Some people have accused me of being too evangelistic; others have accused me of not being evangelistic enough.

You never know how bad the destructive intentions of others will get. I went through a period of time when I was feeling overwhelmed with all the things happening in the church. Great things were taking place, but it was emotionally draining. We had some severe challenges, and I knew I was in over my head. Truthfully, I was discouraged and wondering if it was time for me to leave.

Then one day I was opening the mail and found an oversized manila envelope. I tore open the top and pulled out an elaborate certificate. At first glance my spirit jumped; I thought I'd won some type of award, and such recognition was just the type of positive pick-me-up I needed at that moment. With excitement building, I read the text on the certificate. Big letters in the middle said, "Congratulations to the World's Worst Pastor." Then there was a bunch of text beneath that to explain exactly why I was unfit for the ministry. Some poor guy actually toiled at home for hours making this terrific certificate to tell me what a loser I was. Trust me, if you're doing anything of significance, you'll attract your fair share of antagonists and critics.

One of the most important skills in the pursuit of your cause is knowing how to forgive those who attack you or bad-mouth you. As hard as it is to hear what some say about your good-hearted efforts, you cannot let those derogatory comments and smear tactics derail you. Ultimately you do not answer to your critics; you answer to the One who gave you the cause. All the nastiness shown to me over the years has simply deepened my appreciation for the forgiveness that Jesus Christ has shown toward me and everyone around me. His response is my model. The more I imitate that kind of understanding and love, the more effective I will be at serving Him and the people who so desperately need to be blessed.

One of my advisers helped me get a grip on unfair criticism and the practice of forgiveness. He reminded me that negative reactions often reflect critics' personal disappointment over not being able to accomplish the dreams God has placed in their hearts—or perhaps the dreams they conjured up by themselves and God has chosen to withhold His blessing from. Viewing criticism from that perspective, I can actually feel sorrow for the state of mind that hinders those critics from being a positive, value-adding part of the movement of God's people. It is clear that they, too, have fears and hurts and need to be loved and blessed as much as the people who live in the Echo Park area. Perhaps if God can love them through me—via my reactions to their criticism or even my continued steadfastness in doing good for those among us who are struggling—they can get past their insecurities and anger and participate in the healing of the world around them.

The bottom line is simple: you cannot allow your cause to be derailed by critics. It's appropriate to listen to their complaints because sometimes they are right and other times, even if they aren't, you might learn something about yourself, your cause, or how to better influence the lives of people who don't get it. Consider what they say, and if it resonates, do something about it. If their words do not ring true, thank them for their thoughts and move on. Your cause is too important to be negated by the naysayers. Your passion and commitment cannot be squandered trying to make everybody happy. Focus on the incredible thing God has set aside for you.

Your cause is too important to be negated by the naysayers. Your passion and commitment cannot be squandered trying to make everybody happy.

A pastor told me a story about how the famous evangelist D. L. Moody once dealt with a lady's criticism. After attending an evangelistic service over which Moody presided and at which a number of people gave their lives to Christ, the woman stormed through the crowd to speak with him afterward. She told him all the things he had done wrong and how ineffective he was as an evangelist. Worried that he was not serving God well, Moody was eager to learn from this woman who seemed so sure of herself.

"Please tell me," Moody graciously and humbly asked the woman, "how do you share the gospel with people?"

"I don't," she sniffed pretentiously.

Moody thought for a moment while studying his accuser. "Then forgive me, madam, but I prefer the way I bungle evangelism to the way you avoid it."

Criticism may be God's way of realigning you on the road to influence, or it may be a distraction as you are moving ahead. Develop the discernment to know the difference and respond accordingly.

Once you understand your cause, you are on a grand mission to change the world. Granted, you won't change every life. And you'll probably make more than a few mistakes along the way. Certainly you'll face hardships and challenges as you pursue your cause. Get used to it and get over it. Have enough faith in God's love for you, and in the abilities and resources He has given you, to believe that something great is going to come from your commitment to the cause within you.

WHAT I'VE LEARNED

- Don't expect to grasp the fullness of your cause at first; God will reveal it over time.
- God's timing is perfect. Rely on His timing rather than your own.
- Be prepared to do more than you can humanly do.
- Don't let a lack of resources keep you from moving forward with faith and wisdom. Allow God to fill in the miracle space.
- Past failings do not disqualify you from future success.
- You will be criticized often. When the criticism rings true, use it to improve what you do. When it is off base, ignore it. Either way, keep moving toward your cause.

CHAPTER 7

THE POWER OF A PROPER ATTITUDE

WHEN I THINK about what it takes to see a cause become a life-changing reality, I'm convinced two factors are indispensable: operating in the power of God and having the right attitude.

After my Echo Park experience, I returned to Bethel Temple and began to do my work differently. I realized that instead of moaning about the things I didn't have—a big and growing congregation, a hefty budget for outreach, a staff to whom tasks could be delegated, a property that would permit growth—it was critical to be grateful for what the Lord had already provided me.

When I looked at things from that angle, I recognized that I was only twenty years old and was already blessed with the privilege of serving God in full-time pastoral ministry. I had a usable church building. I was located in an area where the needs were so plentiful that any serious attempt at serving people would almost certainly bear fruit. My father was co-pastoring alongside me, essentially giving me the best mentor anyone could hope for. And God had spoken to me—me, the wet-behind-the-ears, never-been-a-pastor kid who had not even reached the legal age for various adult behaviors—about the cause set aside for me to devote my life to. When I looked at things through a lens of gratitude rather than frustration and disappointment, it was a whole new ball game. I went from grousing about not having the tools I needed to get the job done to praying that I would be able to manage all the resources that had already been entrusted to me.

With that attitude I began making the first of hundreds of radical changes in my thinking and activity. To be more visible and easily accessible, I moved my desk and telephone *outside* the church building, onto the cement porch that was between the church building and the sidewalk. I put a candy jar on that desk and offered candy to the neighborhood kids as they walked by, a ploy to enable me to get to know them and for them to feel comfortable around the white man who was always at the usually vacant building on their street. I waved and called out a greeting to people as they passed by on the street, sometimes in Spanish if that seemed appropriate. Rather than being downcast about the hardship of breaking into their world, I treated it like an adventure that held a great treasure at the end if God would give me favor.

From my seat on the porch, I saw all kinds of things happen in the neighborhood. One was the door-to-door preaching carried out by church people who drove in from other parts of Los Angeles to evangelize the area. Invariably their pitch came down to "repent or go to hell." I watched in fascination as many of the area residents kept accepting Christ with each new visitor. They were anxious to get the pests away from their door and realized that saying yes to their request was the fastest way to rid themselves of the visitors. I knew there had to be a better way. These people were poor, but they weren't stupid.

One afternoon a coworker and I went out for lunch at a nearby Panda Express. While eating fried rice and kung pao chicken, we were discussing ways to advance our cause when a startling impression entered my mind: adopt the block. I had spent many hours on the streets talking to the locals and had knocked on quite a few doors, trying to get to know the people and to invite them to the church. The residents were pleasant but uninterested; they'd been hit up by so many vagrant evangelists and religious representatives that they had little interest in what the new guy was selling.

But this adoption idea was different. We could go from door to door and simply offer to serve people and take care of their needs. Instead of preaching condemnation, we would offer love and practical assistance. We'd be following the admonition of Francis of Assisi: preach the gospel to everyone you meet, and use words only if you must. Love is the best sermon anyone will ever experience.

The more we pondered the idea, the more excited we became. Yanking a napkin from the dispenser, I scribbled down the name "Adopt-A-Block" and a few ideas about how to do it. People would venture out from the church in teams of two, adopting a specific block and committing to visit the same thirty homes each week. The assignment was to build relationships and trust with the residents and to serve in whatever manner was most useful to them.

Love is the best sermon anyone will ever experience.

Our demeanor would be one of graciousness—never forcing ourselves upon anyone, but always seeking the best for them while respecting them and their desires. We would need to keep in mind that this was a privilege, not a chore or obligation; it was a chance to bless others just as we have been blessed. And, of course, it was a way of introducing people to Jesus Christ without threatening or fooling them into a commitment they neither understood nor desired.

That simple idea then became the cornerstone concept for our ministry and the foundational program that enabled Bethel Temple to transition into the Dream Center.

It's a very simple idea, but it's the simplest ideas that work the best and make the biggest difference. Adopt-A-Block is a program that reflects the kind of attitude that delivers results. It is based on commitment to people and consistency in the relationship. It is based on wanting to bring joy and happiness into people's lives and a determination to love them, no matter what.

One of the important aspects of an attitude is that it becomes contagious. People often remark that the Dream Center is such an upbeat, positive place even though we are located in the midst of people whose lives have fallen apart. The optimistic, hopeful feeling doesn't happen by accident. I make a conscious decision every day to set a positive tone for everyone around me. I don't always feel energetic and enthusiastic deep inside, but it's important to project that kind of can-do, victorious spirit for those around me—as well as for myself. If I allow my surroundings to dictate my feelings, before I know it, they'll dictate my outcomes, too.

Part of the challenge is how you describe your setting. At the Dream Center, we have drug addicts, alcoholics, ex-convicts, prostitutes, runaways, pregnant teens, gang members—lots of people who have a history of making bad decisions. It would be easy to look at them and conclude that our work is a burden that must be done and that we're the ones stuck with it. But a more accurate way of defining the situation is to realize that of all the people in the world that God could have chosen for the task, He chose me! It's an honor to be chosen. It looks like a very difficult task, but that He chose me for it and that He never sets me up for failure means He believes I'm the right man for the job and am fully capable of pulling it off. That makes me want to puff out my chest another inch or so—not out of pride but out of the thrill of knowing that He trusts me to do a significant and challenging work that matters to Him.

When we have a new batch of volunteers to introduce to Adopt-A-Block, we do some training with them. One component of the preparation that often stuns people is the emphasis we place upon properly cleaning the sidewalks and streets of the block they will serve. We have a young man named Jonathan who has been with us for a few years. He originally came to the Dream Center because his mother knew he was in trouble and she wanted him to get back on track. His father had left the family when Jonathan was eight, and the youngster immediately began taking advantage of the situation. By age ten he was drinking; by eleven he was smoking marijuana regularly and hanging out with a bad crowd. By age twelve he had started his own gang, and they were spraying graffiti on buildings and vandalizing homes. His gang got to be so big that it was invited to join one of the existing, hard-core gangs. After he turned thirteen, he became a successful drug dealer. Personally, Jonathan was graduating to using as well as selling harder and harder drugs. By age fourteen he was involved in a lot of violence with other gangs whose drug territory he had encroached upon. At age fifteen he was arrested several times, and things were looking bad.

His poor, beleaguered mom was working several jobs, trying to make ends meet while taking care of her three children. She knew Jonathan's life was a mess but was at a loss about what to do. The kids had taken over the house and were both using and selling drugs there. She found out about the Dream Center and decided to take Jonathan there in the hopes of having his life reclaimed. Jonathan remembers it well:

> It was October 26. She had me in the car, and we drove out to the Dream Center. We rolled up to the campus, and I looked at that big building and thought, *Oh no, she's putting me in a psychiatric hospital.* My mom was freaking out because this was so hard for her. She's from Mexico and doesn't always

understand everything so well either. And I was freaking out but thinking I'd figure this place out and work the system. I had snuck some weed into my boxer shorts, figuring they'd never search me there, and they didn't find it, so I was excited. I hid the weed, then just lay low for a few days, taking the measure of the place, figuring out who the snitches were, who the key dudes were, the whole deal.

After four days I was ready. I stole a toaster from the kitchen, ripped a page out of the Bible my mother gave me when she left, and rolled a joint in that page and lit it with the toaster. I had my head out the window so people inside wouldn't smell anything, and it all seemed cool to me. I hid the rest of the weed. The next day I returned to smoke another joint, but my stash was gone. Then the house leader came down on me and told me they were busting me to Level 1, which is for the bad dudes and has a lot of restrictions. So I spent a lot of time sitting in my room, bored, counting the spots on the ceiling and stuff like that. I could hear everyone else laughing at the movies or chillin' in the halls, but on Level 1 you can't do that, so it was really horrible. Finally, I was so bored I picked up that Bible and decided to read it.

So I went to the restroom and was sitting on the toilet when I started reading the Bible. I opened it up to Matthew 5, which is the beginning of the Sermon on the Mount. Now I did not know anything in the Bible, so this was all news to me. Right away, it changed me—man, what Jesus was saying just blew my mind. It was the first time I'd ever heard anyone say that if I even *looked* at a woman the wrong way, I've already committed adultery in my heart.[11] Say what? I was thinking, *Wait a minute, nobody ever told me anything like this!* Then I read that if I kept anger toward

someone in my heart it was like murdering them. I'm sure I
didn't understand all of the ideas I was reading, but the one
thing that was clear was that whoever wrote that book took
everything to a higher standard. This Jesus guy just took
everything to a new level.

I was shocked. I felt, *Man, if I'd never read any of this I'd
be okay, but now? I read it already.* I have to say, that was a
defining moment in my life, right there in the men's room
with that Bible. So I was thinking about all this, and I made a
decision. I just said to myself, *Jesus, I'm going to serve you.
I'm going to serve you with my whole heart.*

Jonathan then went through our discipleship process and became
an amazing leader for others who came from the streets. During the
holiday break he went home for the first time since his decision to
follow Christ. That same day he broke up with his old girlfriend,
threw out about a pound of marijuana he had hidden in his mother's
house, and told his old gang buddies that he was out of that life for
good. His heart had been so radically changed that he could imagine
no other course of action. He told God that he was committing his
life to the Kingdom and would serve however God desired. That was
a huge step for Jonathan. Once you leave a gang, there's no return.
But he was committed to loving God and people. His entire attitude
changed. And what I love about him was his fervor for doing the
right things the right way for the right reasons. He became a floor
leader in the discipleship program, he finished his GED, and then
we made him the director of the Adopt-A-Block program. Part of the
reason was his leadership skills; people really respond to him. But the
primary reason was his attitude:

I fell in love with serving. I started dreaming about what it
would be like if one day I could love these people so much

THE CAUSE WITHIN YOU

that they ask, what's different about me? There's nothing better than when someone asks what's different about you, without you ever having told them about Jesus. I love it when they get that look, like they're thinking, *I don't know, man, there's something different about you.*

You serve them without being asked, and they start asking things, like, "Hey, why'd you carry my luggage for me?" "Why'd you help me with that task?" "Why'd you pay for that?" That's something I learned from Matthew Barnett; he's always thinking like this. Like, he'll go through a drive-through and pay for the person behind him. So you start thinking up ways to be generous, ways to be a blessing, ways to serve. The number-one thing I've learned here is to be aware and conscious of what's going on around me so I can be a blessing. I'm always trying to be aware so that when the moment is there, I can drop seeds of blessing.

They made me a leader of the youth group, and then one day, out of nowhere, they asked me to run the Adopt-A-Block program. I was not quite twenty years old at the time. I couldn't believe it. Adopt-A-Block is not just the first ministry they got going, it's also my favorite. I couldn't believe it; I was totally shocked. I was just finishing high school at that point. They trained me and taught me a lot of new skills, especially administration skills, which were my weakness. Since I've been running the program, we have doubled our number of volunteers to about 600 coming to serve each week, and we're serving about 30,000 people per week, which is also up. It's just cool to see God at work.

What's crazy to me is how much they have believed in me and encouraged me. Now my whole goal in life is to love people and to love God. Like, I want to love people so much that I connect them to Jesus. I want to meet not only their spiritual needs, but also their physical needs. One thing that Pastor Matthew has convinced me of is that I'm here to speak into people's potential.

That is what they did with me. Pastor Matthew Barnett and some of the leaders here came into my life and spoke into my potential. They kept telling me, "You're a man of God. You can be a great leader one day." I was like, "What? Me? Really?" But when you hear it over and over from people you watch and respect, you start believing those things for yourself. It made me realize that if I had that potential, then I'd better learn to serve better. They spoke so much to my potential that I started to believe in myself and take steps to turn that potential into performance.

Being here, with all I've been through, now I realize that I have a heart for LA. I was born and raised here. They are my peeps, right here. I get excited about serving here. That's my goal, to serve these people, right here in this neighborhood.

I brought up Jonathan's story because he is a stellar example of someone who leads others to recognize the privilege of being called by God to do even the most menial tasks. Jonathan is a great motivator who helps people take pride in everything they do. Those of us who conduct a lot of the training for servants work hard at reshaping people's perspective about what it means to be a servant. For Adopt-A-Block, we typically pick up all the trash on the streets and sidewalks and vacant lots in the neighborhoods we serve. A lot of people normally think of that as scut work, a task meant for the lowliest of the low. We try to elevate the importance of that task by helping people realize they're not picking up garbage; they're restoring respectability to the place where God's beloved people live. They are rebuilding people's dignity by providing them with a beautiful place to live. They are demonstrating their love by doing something that many people would turn up their noses at.

Our lives are lived in the midst of a raging spiritual battle for people's hearts and souls. The battle is won by love delivered through service. That's what Jesus modeled for us; our job is to imitate His example every chance we get. Instead of allowing our servants to think of the garbage collection time as the despised, gotta-get-through-this phase of their day on the block, it should be a time in which we joyfully and proudly remove every last piece of refuse that might signal that someone other than precious, highly esteemed people live in the area. There is nothing more important for us to do in that area than rid it of any vestige of filth or imperfection.

> **Our lives are lived in the midst of a raging spiritual battle for people's hearts and souls.**

What we are doing is building an attitude. And I have to admit, that attitude becomes contagious. When our people initially adopt a block and spend an hour or two collecting every last bit of trash and rubble, the people in the neighborhood watch us as if we were a bunch of crazy people on holiday from the local psychiatric ward. They dismiss us as nuts. The second week, we repeat the process, and they watch in wonder. The third week, a few of them thank us. The fourth week, some of the residents join us. By the time we're into our second month of this cleansing and visiting routine, they know us, expect us, see the love we're bringing to them with no strings attached, and not only accept us but serve alongside us and befriend us. Often after a couple months of this, there's not much garbage to pick up on their streets because now they, too, take pride in their place of residence. Their attitude has been affected in a positive and permanent way.

Part of the process of changing your attitude is to train yourself to see the positive side of every situation. When Bethel Temple was struggling and nobody was attending, my dad and I did not give up. One Sunday, in fact, he flew into Los Angeles after he'd preached in

Phoenix, and we prayed in that sanctuary until nearly dawn, asking for God's blessing and a breakthrough. Then one week we had five people show up. I was ecstatic. The next week we had maybe eight people, and I was ready to do backflips. My dad and I would talk on Mondays about how our weekends had gone. "Dad, I had a great weekend. I had eight people!" And my dad really celebrated that with me; he was genuinely jazzed about the growth that was taking place. High with this success, I'd casually ask how his church had done. "It was great; we had eight thousand this weekend." I could have immediately clammed up and felt nauseated over the disparity. But we were pulling for each other, knowing that the numbers were not the real measure of success and that we were on the same team anyway, both serving a great God who was blessing each of us in His own way.

As time went on I had more and more positive outcomes to celebrate. We opened up our recovery program and helped a half dozen drunks get Jesus and get sober. We opened up our first drug recovery house and helped a dozen addicts get off the junk and on to Jesus. We had a group from another church visit our campus for the first time to see what we were doing with the invisible people of the city. I remember taking them on a quick tour of our cramped, small facilities. I'd open the door of a room that was eight feet by eight feet. Our visitors saw a tiny room with marked-up white walls, a few school desks, and a bunch of chairs; I saw a tutoring center and described the life-changing work that took place in that humble space.

When we started giving out food to hungry people, I paid for the food out of pocket because the church had no money. My first day on the streets dispensing food was in the company of Fred Johnson, a one-legged military vet who was the first person willing to accompany me on the street to distribute the food. We celebrated the privilege of giving away food to about twenty people.

All those experiences taught me a crucial lesson: *learn to love the stage you're in.* Maybe bigger and better things will come to you in the future; maybe they won't. It doesn't matter. Appreciate the honor and the opportunities God has given you in the moment. He is master of the future, not you, and you really cannot dictate what the future will be, so flow with Him. Enjoy the journey. If you're always looking ahead and yearning to reach the final destination, you'll miss the beauty and joy that comes from experiencing things along the way. When you finally reach the destination, it will seem empty and pointless unless you've appreciated the little victories en route to the destination. See the positive side of each situation.

When people visit the Dream Center, one of the most common questions raised is how we keep from becoming discouraged over all the people who enter our recovery programs and don't make it. My answer is that I choose to think about the ones who do make it— those whose lives have been reclaimed and who now have a dream that they live to carry out. The ones who relapse are works in progress; God is not done with them yet, and we are always ready and waiting to love them some more. If I focused mainly on the dropouts, it would become depressing, and I'd become paralyzed by those setbacks. Then we would stop doing good works because we did not have a perfect track record, and where would that leave things? Are we better off helping some and praying for the future healing of the remainder, or seeing a few failures and closing down the shop? Your attitude is a choice. I've chosen to focus on and celebrate the miracles God is performing around us rather than be dragged down by the substantial number of people who have yet to be healed and to embrace their life's cause.

For years I've been joining our teams every Saturday for the Adopt-A-Block activities. One weekend, early in the process, I visited the home of an elderly Filipino man. Max was in his eighties, his family was no longer alive, and he was basically waiting to die. He opened his front door after I knocked, we exchanged greetings, and he inquired as to what I wanted. After explaining that I was from a church and we were there to serve him, I asked if there was anything I could do to help him. Max said no, paused, then said that he hadn't been to church in a long time. He paused again, then asked if I could come into his home and read the Bible to him.

His home was very basic, but Max made me take his easy chair and he sat across from me attentively and waited. I began reading 1 Corinthians 13, the chapter about love. When I finished, Max sat there for a few moments looking at me. "Will you come back every week and talk to me about this?" he asked. I agreed, and for the next ten weeks or so we did a Bible study about love. During our times together, this lonely war veteran poured his heart out to me, and we had some terrific discussions. At the end of the ten weeks, I told Max that now it was his turn. His assignment was to find somebody to love by serving them during the coming week.

When I visited Max the following Saturday, I knocked on his front door, and he answered it quickly. He put his fingers to his lips and said, "Pastor, shhh!" I stole a quick glance behind me and to both sides, wondering what was going on. He explained. "You told me to love someone, to serve somebody this week, right? Well, I was walking home from the market, and I saw a homeless family living on the street. They had just crossed the border and had no place to go. They're inside now, the whole family."

I looked over Max's shoulder, into his living room, and saw them. There was a mother and father with two young children. They had no shoes, and their clothing was ragged. The children seemed especially dirty and disheveled. They looked like poster children for World Vision. Max continued, "They've been walking for days. They sneaked over the border and walked all the way up here. They have no relatives or friends around. I invited them to stay with me."

He looked over my shoulder into the street, then whispered again. "But, Pastor, you have to be quiet because they're illegal." I laughed and said, "Max, don't worry, we've got about two million illegal people in this neighborhood!" I know the political issues surrounding illegal immigration are real, and I didn't mean to diminish their significance, but his worry seemed humorous, given the population of our section of Los Angeles.

He pulled me into his home, and we looked at this family, lying on his carpeted floor. "Pastor, they need clothes. Do you have any clothes for them?" I was so proud of Max. Here was this isolated old man who now had something worthwhile to live for. I'd told him about God's love, then Max had gone out and shared God's love with people he'd never even seen. What a chain reaction this could cause.

By the grace of God, the Dream Center had just received a truckload of high-quality, expensive Guess jeans that had been donated to our clothing distribution center. From Max's living room, I called our team at the clothing room, explained what we needed, and a while later they arrived with several sacks of clothes to outfit everyone in the family. The family got all kinds of new clothes—jackets, jeans, shirts and blouses, shoes and sneakers, even underwear and socks.

As we handed them all these things, the father started crying. Then in Spanish he explained to his family what was happening. By the time he was done, the rest of them were crying too. Then the father said, "I have just arrived in America, and one man has given me a place to live, and a church has clothed my entire family. I love this country! Is everybody in America like this?"

We're working on it. . . .

Related to your attitude is your definition of success. The goals you set for your cause will naturally relate to what you think of as success. Realizing this revolutionized my life.

Because I come from two generations of pastors, my inclination was to see numbers as the most effective measure of success. Research conducted by The Barna Group shows that such a perspective about success is the norm among pastors. The typical pastor measures success according to five indicators: how many people attend church services, how much money is raised for ministry, how many staff members are hired, how many programs are active, and how much square footage has been built for ministry activities.

All of that is fine, but none of it is what Jesus died for. He died for the well-being of people—to see their lives totally transformed by love and verified by their own acts of service. The real measure of success, then, is obedience to God's principles and calling. Success is about influencing lives, which requires us to be mission minded. Put differently, success is a by-product of your hard work that bears fruit for the cause that God placed within you.

America has a success-crazed culture. Sadly, too few people view success through God's eyes, preferring to chase it according to society's perspective. People are constantly chasing success but never achieving it. Why? Because success in our culture is a moving target. Yet the quest for success becomes so seductive that it blends with our personal values and self-image, resulting in lofty ambitions.

Ambition is a key factor. It is all about self. It emphasizes getting credit for outcomes, establishing a unique and high-profile identity, getting ahead, and defeating others against whom you compete. Mission is almost the polar opposite. Mission is about the cause, and it doesn't take account of who gets credit or fame. When you're invested in a mission, you submit to others, serve whenever possible, and stay engaged in the battle, no matter how difficult it becomes. People motivated by ambition often walk away from the battle when it gets too tough, looking for something that's easier to master. Those driven by ambition are all about making it big. Those who focus on their causes want to help others do well.

The whole emphasis on success has nestled its way into almost every nook and cranny of our society, including many of our churches. It can be deceiving. Several years ago I was invited to speak at the leadership conference that draws the largest attendance of any church-oriented leadership event each year. I felt honored to be there and excited to share what we had discovered about leadership in the context of a servant culture.

When you're invested in a mission, you submit to others, serve whenever possible, and stay engaged in the battle, no matter how difficult it becomes.

But as I sat in that huge auditorium and listened with rapt attention to the superb speakers who preceded me, I became increasingly nervous. They discussed all kinds of sophisticated strategies and tactics they employed to grow their church attendance and to expand their program base. They described, in detail, extensive plans and complex models. They talked about how they were gearing up for conditions they anticipated in the future. My head was swimming! Clearly those brothers were captivating speakers and brilliant leaders. You could easily see why people would be attracted to their churches.

As it got close to the time for me to follow them onstage, I was a wreck. I sneaked into the restroom and started weeping. I was completely intimidated. Locked into one of the stalls, I silently prayed to God, *Lord, I don't know how to be a success. I don't know a model of success. I don't know what to talk about to these people. I don't belong here. Please help me. I don't have any success strategies to share with them.*

As He always seems to do, God bailed me out. He replied, *That's exactly what I want you to speak on. Preach about the fact that you are not called to be a success and that your work is not measured by the world's standards or models. Describe the simplicity of your ministry with boldness. Tell them that your calling is simple: you just want to be a blessing to everyone you meet.*

So that became the title of the presentation: "I Don't Want to Be a Success." Speaking from my heart and experience, I explained that none of us will know if we're a success until we get to heaven anyway. After all, we don't see things the way God does, so how could we really measure it? And if we cannot measure or gauge it, why stress over it and wrap our lives around it? God has given us a cause to focus upon, and that cause is always about helping people; it is never about how successful we can set ourselves up to become. When you set your mind on the things of God—that is, loving people and giving Him the glory—you are liberated from the stresses and snares of the world. If you have influence, use it to make a difference by helping people.

No doubt many of the people who heard me that day felt I was the low point of the program; I did not provide them with a three-point plan to follow or suggest an innovative model for structuring ministry. Don't misunderstand; I have nothing against all the carefully developed plans and multifaceted models the other speakers described. I would not tell people they have misinterpreted God's cause or have embraced an errant approach to fulfilling it by using such models. God may well use them through those means, and that may well be the approach that works for them in their context.

Perhaps my presentation that day was meant solely for my own edification. If so, it worked! I left there feeling personally freed from the burden of having to compete against anyone else in order to become a success. That day it became clear that it would be possible to devote my entire life to achieving what people might point to and label as success and still be unfulfilled. As I thought about it, I realized you can lose yourself in that special cause God gives you and never even think about how that effort relates to the world's version of success. You can get so wrapped up in loving and serving that success falls off the radar. Believe me, having transitioned from the kid with ulcers at age twenty to a guy in his midthirties who doesn't have a clue where this will all wind up—or really care—I can tell you that chasing success isn't all it's cracked up to be. Focus on faithfully pursuing your cause, and don't worry about persuading the world that you're a success. You'll never miss it.

Let me offer a final word about cultivating the right attitude: do your homework.

Probably the best lessons I learn are those that occur in the trenches—or in my case, on the streets. There is no substitute for experience. But you can significantly sharpen your performance by getting useful information and advice ahead of time. Doing your homework regarding your cause and the people you serve is not only good stewardship; it also shows that you have enough respect for the people you are serving that you go out of your way to do your very best. When you wing it, the message you send is equally clear: the task didn't justify your time and effort.

Remember Alena Strickland, the mother who takes in sick children and raises them? Before she began serving those children, Alena spent hour after hour memorizing medical terminology, studying basic medical care procedures, passing tests for emergency medical techniques, getting training on how to operate the complex machines those children required, learning how to diagnose symptoms—the list goes on. Many people put in her situation might have thought they were doing a heroic work simply by bringing those children into their homes and being kind to them. Alena realized that kindness is deeper than a smile and good intentions; it demands a wholehearted effort to care for others in the way they need to be cared for. She fully invested herself in becoming an expert in caring for children suffering from all kinds of difficulties. When you speak to some of the medical professionals who refer children to her, you get an appreciation for the commitment she has made to being the best at what she does.

No matter how well you research your cause and the challenges you'll face, you will make mistakes. You cannot let that hold you back. Devote yourself to diligence rather than perfection. Invest in reasonable self-improvement, but don't obsess over your inadequacies. Get as much information as you need to advance your ability to serve well, without falling prey to analysis paralysis.

My assistant, Todd, is a great example of someone who always does his homework thoroughly. For instance, when I take a trip somewhere, usually to speak at a church or conference, Todd puts together all the details of my trip. When I am ready to leave the office, he has investigated everything I am likely to face during my journey and provides me with detailed instructions about everything. For each city I go to, he'll have an hour-by-hour itinerary, with the names and backgrounds of people I might encounter; the location of the kinds of restaurants I would enjoy, in case I go out for a meal; how to travel from one location to the next; details about my accommodations; and so forth. One of the highly successful businesspeople in our congregation walked me to my car one day as I was about to leave on such a trip. He looked at the folder Todd had prepared for my journey—it was probably a forty-page document for my three-day trip—and his jaw fell open. I have a feeling some changes were made at his office after I left town.

Todd says his cause is to prepare me to lead people as I pursue the cause God has given me. He loves our cause of restoring broken lives in the city through the love of Christ and power of servanthood—and he loves enabling me to be freed and ready to do what needs to be done to further those ends. He has become an extension of my work. For a decade we have worked shoulder to shoulder to serve all kinds of people in all kinds of situations. I am able to do what I do in part because of the commitment Todd has made to doing his homework on my behalf—all because he can see how it translates into the fulfillment of a great cause.

You need to have that same sense of obligation so that you can perform at your highest level. The people you will serve deserve nothing less.

WHAT I'VE LEARNED

- Without the right attitude, your cause will not get out of the starting gate.
- Accentuate the positive.
- Focus your attention on God and people; nothing else really matters.
- Be encouraged by every little sign of progress.
- Attitudes are contagious.
- Do not become ambitious for success; become obedient in the pursuit of your cause.
- Do your homework.

CHAPTER 8

GET IT DONE

WE HAD BEEN TALKING for a few months about initiating a live-in program for poor families at the Dream Center. We had gone so far as to identify the people who had a passion for the cause and had talked about what space we might be able to develop for families. We were on track to get that program off the ground in perhaps six months' time, when we believed the housing space would be ready and we would be able to free up the staff who were passionate about managing the process.

But God rarely respects our calendars, and I believe He often tests us to see if we're serious about doing what we claim we want to do. One day, without warning and months before we felt we'd be ready to launch a family program, we received a call from the police about a family that had moved here from Boston with six young children. Everything they had lined up prior to their move west fell apart once they were here, and they had no cushion to ease their fall. The police have gotten used to working with us. They knew that other social agencies would take time to process the paperwork and that the downtown missions would have to split up the family.

Knowing the dire realities the family faced, we invited the police to bring them to our campus. We shifted into overdrive and quickly created a place for them to stay. During their time with us, we helped them prepare for a successful reentry into the marketplace by providing job training, babysitting, résumé preparation, and more. The timing wasn't ideal for us, but poverty and living on the streets weren't exactly ideal for them, either. Their need trumped our desire for a perfect launch. And that unexpected entry into family assistance triggered a ministry that now houses more than a hundred people from over two dozen families who are working hard to become independent and self-reliant once again.

The launch of our family program is just one of many instances when we've jumped into action ahead of schedule. Perhaps that's why, though I'm not someone who regularly gives free commercial plugs, I am a fan of the famous Nike slogan: Just Do It. It's a hallmark of our work at the Dream Center. Sure, we want to think things through and be as well-prepared as feasible before we act to ensure we are efficient and effective. But in the end, it's all for nothing if we don't put the engine in gear and get things rolling.

One of the phrases I use to motivate our people to action is that we have to *think big and act small*. What that means is that God has given us a big cause—bigger than we can handle on our own and bigger than we can fulfill quickly. So what we have to do is act small— that is, engage in a series of small steps that add up to big impact. (The truth is that there is no such thing as a "small step"—every step matters, so if it is productive, it is significant. But the contrast of accomplishing a big dream through a series of small steps sticks in people's minds better than telling them something like "do whatever you must to get the results you want.")

Every great dream takes a long time and a lot of effort to fulfill, so the keys to progress are courage and consistency. Each step forward may feel so small that it seems insignificant, but when you put them all together, the results are surprising. One of my friends in ministry told me about his efforts to lead churches through substantial change in the way they do outreach. He was constantly discouraged because he couldn't seem to find the one big thing that would cause thousands of churches to grasp the need and make the required shifts in thinking and behavior. He says he finally woke up to the idea that the best strategy was just to keep plodding along, enabling one church to get it and change, and then a second one, and then a third, slowly building momentum. If he remained diligent in pursuing the cause to which he was committed, eventually an entire movement would be in place. And that's exactly how it works: you help change one life at a time, and if you are sufficiently persistent, you eventually find that many lives have been changed, one at a time.

That really has been the story of the Dream Center. We started with a big dream and made it a reality by implementing small step after small step. We discovered that people needed food, so I bought food out of my own salary to hand out to people. The needs continued to expand, so I gave more money from my salary. The needs grew bigger, beyond what I could afford personally, so we asked a few stores to help by donating some food. The needs multiplied, so we got a crew of volunteers on the phones asking more stores to donate food. Today we distribute more than one million pounds of food every month, with dozens of stores donating food, from major grocery store chains like Albertsons to some local mom-and-pop convenience stores who want to invest in their neighborhood.

That food program, by the way, grew larger because the more we understood the extent of the need and devoted ourselves to meeting that need, the greater our sense of urgency became to get the job done. Without urgency, it's easy to be lethargic about the tasks demanding effort. Without urgency, why strain your brain to come up with creative solutions? Without urgency, why turn to God in fervent prayer, begging Him to honor you with the resources you need to bless people? Without urgency, your focus wanders to other, more enticing opportunities. If you don't feel a sense of urgency about your cause, something's wrong. You need to do a self-evaluation and figure out if you are really committed to the cause or just playing at it. If you are committed, you should have the passion of urgency burning within you, recognizing that if you cannot get the job done, people will suffer.

Progress and impact are based on consistency. When you are fully focused on your cause and pulling out all the stops to get it done, those small steps accumulate and build momentum, which becomes like a freight train. Once you get momentum rolling in your favor, it's hard to stop. I look at people's efforts to fulfill their causes and search for evidence of momentum because if they have it, they're going to be fine. If momentum is missing or has stalled out, then there's a problem that needs to be addressed.

Sometimes a cause never gets rolling because the ultimate objectives or measures of significance are wrong. For instance, many churches never become effective because their goal is to attract a specific number of people to attend their services. Based on the energy devoted to that central goal, one would have to assume that the heartbeat of their cause relates to increasing their attendance. Now who is going to come up alongside of you and get excited about filling seats? Who cares about that? But if you strive to bring together like-minded people who want to exercise God's power and follow His principles in healing broken lives, then you've given people a cause worth disrupting their lives to pursue. Pursuing bigness, whether it's for a church, a business, a nonprofit organization, or anything else, is a distraction; increased size should be a by-product of delivering something that people really need at a level of quality that respects the intended recipients. Establishing bigness as a goal simply puts pressure and stress on you and diverts your attention from investing yourself and others in the things that matter: changed lives.

Our Adopt-A-Block program is running smoothly and blessing thousands of households in our area. I believe we will continue expanding our territory to the point that someday we will bless every home in Hollywood, too. Every time I look out my office window at that famous Hollywood sign in the not-too-distant hills, my heart leaps with excitement at the thought of reaching every home between our campus and the outer reaches of Hollywood. But I know that to do so, we have to keep taking one small step forward at a time. It's the consistency of taking the appropriate intermediate steps that will result in a big impact.

If you strive to bring together like-minded people who want to exercise God's power and heal broken lives, then you've given people a cause worth disrupting their lives to pursue.

Don't get caught in the cycle of talking an issue to death before you try to solve it. I've met with plenty of leaders who marvel at how quickly the Dream Center swings into action. It never dawned on me that we were doing anything unusual, so I used to ask why they hadn't done the same thing. Variations on the same story were given time after time: the need for multiple levels of meetings, the need to develop procedural manuals and training systems, the need to test the process, the need to raise the budget before starting out, and so forth. I think that such regimented expectations might make sense if you're creating a new flavor of ice cream or experimenting with a new way of building a carburetor. But if you're pursuing God's cause, which always relates to blessing people, often there is no time to lose in alleviating their suffering.

Our mentality at the Dream Center is "first solve the need, then discuss it." I will concede that this is not always the most efficient way of approaching a task, but when people's lives are on the line, it makes more sense to learn on the job than to wait until you are capable of initiating a flawless process. Our priority is to help people, and one of our guiding principles is to treat other people the way we'd want to be treated. I know if I were addicted to drugs, or trying to escape from a life of prostitution, or trying to find a way to get my family off the streets, I would not want to wait while a group of well-intentioned people tried to create the perfect solution. In my desperation, even a half-baked solution would probably be better than nothing; it's certainly a risk I'd take. Knowing there was a group of people who cared about me and would remain committed to working with me as they sought to improve their level of service would be a huge blessing.

Our mentality at the Dream Center is "first solve the need, then discuss it."

A great example of acting on a need before debating its fine points was our involvement with people who lost everything in the aftermath of Hurricane Katrina. That devastation became an international headline for weeks. Churches from around the country sent teams of people to the New Orleans area to help. We had many people travel there too. But the need in Louisiana was overwhelming. There were thousands of people living in temporary shelters set up in places like the Superdome. Meanwhile, tens of thousands stayed in their waterlogged, unsafe homes waiting for help. Those people would never recover any of their things—homes, cars, clothing, family mementos, prized possessions, even friends and family members. Many of them had been on the edge financially before the storm hit. Now they were jobless, penniless, homeless, and in many cases hopeless.

We were able to arrange for several private planes to head to Louisiana to bring back three hundred of the displaced victims. We flew them to Los Angeles and arranged places for them to stay on our campus. We provided free housing, meals, clothing, and medical care. We put together a job fair, where twenty-nine area employers met with evacuees who were interested in pursuing employment opportunities. We arranged for their children to be schooled. Government agencies set up shop on our campus to assist in the provision of benefits directly to those families.

We promised—and provided—this kind of care for twelve months. We did not corner them with gospel presentations or tracts or require attendance at church services in order for them to receive shelter and their basic necessities. Our objective was to love them back to health and stability. It was an offer of unconditional, no-strings-attached love.

Of course, we had no way of knowing that Katrina was coming or how disastrous it would be, so none of this outreach activity was in our plans or budget. We were already struggling to make ends meet financially, but we could not turn our backs on people in need. When the tragedy struck, we did not have an emergency board meeting, followed by executive meetings, management meetings, and operational meetings to debate the wisdom of this involvement. We did not take a congregational vote to make sure church members were comfortable with our participation in the relief effort. There were no interns dispatched to the library to pull together facts about previous disasters and how churches had responded to the need. We did not make a series of phone calls to quiz experts regarding the pros and cons of engagement to determine if we should act. We never sought the support of our denomination nor sponsored a survey to gauge the potential impact on our public image as a means to figuring out whether we should get involved.

People's lives had been shattered and they needed help. Our cause is to restore broken lives. There really wasn't anything to discuss.

Of course, once we got the survivors out of Louisiana and into

Los Angeles, we had plenty to discuss. But by that time they had a comfortable if basic place to live, new clothing that fit them, three hot meals a day, access to transportation, and they were well on their way to rebuilding their lives. So while my team and I huddled to consider the related operational issues, the lives of our guests from New Orleans were already being put back together.

I can only speak from personal experience, but my history shows that God always provides what you need when you are faithful to Him and the great cause He planted within you. When word got out that we had flown in three hundred survivors, hundreds of generous people lined up to help us assist our new guests. Cars and trucks snaked their way around the block of our campus for several days, filled with compassionate people of all faiths and ethnicities who went out of their way to drop off food and supplies. Many others stopped by or sent in cash donations to help defray some of the costs. Some people called us to sponsor a family for several months.

God always provides what you need when you are faithful to Him and the great cause He planted within you.

Pay attention to what your conscience tells you. That's one of the ways God speaks to you and moves you. Inside you know the right thing to do. The challenge is to muster the courage to move forward and the determination to be persistent. Just don't waste your time arguing with people about the mechanics of how, where, why, and when. Get on with it. Serve people and listen for God's direction.

Another example of the importance of listening to God, reading the signs of your circumstances, and then stepping up to do what's right is our recent work with women who have been enslaved in sex trafficking. This is an issue that has received lots of attention over the past five years. In fact, it garnered so much media coverage and was talked about by so many leaders that I assumed it was a problem for which there were plenty of existing solutions. I used to follow the conversations on Facebook and Twitter about the issue and believed it must be well covered, given all the chatter and authoritative conversation about helping sex-traffic victims.

Boy, was I wrong!

A couple of people in our ministry expressed their desire for us to be involved in rescuing girls from being sold and used as sex slaves, and the facts they shared with me were shocking. Although it is estimated that more than 16,000 people are victims of the sex-traffic industry—and at least 1,000 of those are in Los Angeles—the entire country had only thirty-nine sanctioned spaces for girls rescued from that life. Los Angeles had only a handful of safe, officially sanctioned places for those girls to escape to. There was a lot of awareness but little action.

Not long after our conversation about this social ill, we had an opportunity to rescue our first girl from the sex-traffic trade. We picked her up and brought her to a secret location where she would be cared for and secure. Since then we have increased the number of girls rescued and have become one of the primary sanctioned spots to which sex-trafficked girls can escape.

That first young woman we helped, Karen, told us the chilling tale of her life and why it was so important that we came to her aid:

> I don't remember a time in my life when I was not being sexually abused. My father started abusing me when I was five. At the age of ten, he sold me to someone for $2,000. He gave legal papers to my new owner and everything, just like you would if you were buying a car or some other commodity. I thought it must be normal.
>
> The next ten years were hell. I was made to have sex with all kinds of people. There were months at a time when I was

locked in a cage in someone's basement and forced to have sex with him. Many of these men were middle-class guys from nice, respectable neighborhoods. You'd be surprised how common sex trafficking is in what people assume to be good areas.

By the time I was sixteen, I had learned the whole business and was running a couple of houses for my daddy—that's what the girls call the man who bought them. I had two houses, each with about twelve or thirteen girls, and I was in charge of breaking the girls and overseeing them. Breaking them means you strip them down emotionally to nothing; you take away their self-worth and self-esteem so that you can build them back up to whatever you want them to be. They become your slave. They'll do whatever you want them to do. It's really sick, I see that now, but when I was in it, it just seemed completely natural and normal. It was just business.

There was a lot of physical violence and drugs involved. My daddy, or pimp, used to beat me up pretty bad, and he often used electrical shock on me. I go to a neurologist now because I have a lot of nerve damage and I'm in constant pain. It's kind of hard for me to walk, but I hope that some of this will heal over time. I'm always tired. My body needs to recover from all the years of abuse it's been through.

My pimp even brainwashed me, although I didn't realize it at the time. He used the Bible to do it. He would read parts of the Bible to me over and over and interpret them in ways that made him seem like he was being really good to me. "I will never leave you nor forsake you."[12] "I created you and formed you and made you who you are."[13] So now, working with the Dream Center, I hear some of these verses and I get really confused. But that was his goal, I guess, to try to keep me from leaving him and being helped by Christians.

When I couldn't stand the abuse anymore and decided to get out, I met a woman who had been a junkie and a prostitute. She talked to me about getting out. At first when I tried to leave, my pimp threatened my family, so I stayed on. But then one day he brought in a new fifteen-year-old and told me to turn her out—you know, break her down and get her ready—and I just couldn't do it. I don't know why, but I couldn't. Somehow I changed from seeing it as business to no longer seeing the girls as commodities to sell. I started to see us as people and knew I had to get out.

We were blessed with the opportunity to help her escape, and Karen is recovering from her former life and preparing for her next phase of life. She is working through all the abuse and even the brainwashing she received. And thankfully, she has a clear sense of her dream, which is, as she says, "to educate people to know how to help someone like me." You'd better believe we will do everything humanly possible to support her in pursuing that dream.

But imagine what would have happened to her if we had waited to debate the readiness of our organization to handle a delicate and difficult recovery program that girls like Karen need. Again, as in the case of the Katrina rescue effort, we did not have the budget, the space, or the expertise to make it happen. But we did what we had to in the moment, and we have seen God do incredible things in response.

Our approach will probably never be written up as a Harvard Business School case study. I can live with that.

To be effective in your pursuit of the cause God has given you, you have to earn the right to be heard. Some people assume that because they are seeking to help others—especially people who are struggling—they automatically have the right to a hearing from those people. You'll quickly find out that's not the case. Americans are suspicious of the motives of others. We typically assume you have no business butting your nose into our business until you have proved yourself worthy of our attention and respect.

How do you earn that opportunity? By getting involved and staying involved. You cannot hope to win people's trust unless you stick around for the long haul. At that point you transition from being an outsider to being "one of us." That's when you have leverage. Until then your motives will remain suspect and your opportunities few and far between.

You cannot hope to win people's trust unless you stick around for the long haul.

Nikki, a young woman who wound up leaving prostitution and completing our recovery program, attended our services every week. Though she has a slight build, one look into her eyes reveals her inner steeliness and strength. In fact, she has seen and overcome a lot in life, and she is not one to back down.

One Sunday I preached about the necessity of dreaming up creative ways to reach people. After the service, she approached me and told me she had a new ministry she wanted to start. I was pleased and asked her what she had in mind. She hesitated and said she was pretty sure we didn't have this ministry already. Knowing we had nearly two hundred different types of ministry in place, I wasn't so sure, so I asked her again to describe what she was thinking about. Finally she said, "It's a pimp ministry." I looked at her a bit funny and asked, "What's that?" She said, like I was stupid, "It's a ministry to pimps." And I had to admit, that was one outreach we did not already have underway. So I asked her what a pimp ministry would entail.

Seeing that she had both my attention and interest, she lit up and went into an explanation of a pimp ministry. "Well, I used to be a prostitute, so I know where they hang out. I go to the donut shop where all the pimps meet on Friday night. Pastor, this is what I do. I open the Bible, and I teach and preach to all the pimps." Besides being shocked, I was truly impressed. At a bit of a loss for words, but hoping to encourage her, I asked her if the pimps liked her preaching and teaching in the donut shop. She got an indignant look on her face and said, "Of course not; they hate it. But you told us we're supposed to tell people about Jesus whether they like it or not."

I felt the muscles in my smiling face tighten. I felt awful. I didn't remember saying that, but perhaps I did in a moment when I got carried away onstage, speaking about the importance of bringing people to Jesus, or maybe she misinterpreted something I had said, taking it out of context. Not wanting to burst her bubble or destroy her courage, I simply said, "Well, praise the Lord, Nikki. May God go with you as you go. I won't go with you, but may He be with you as you go."

So feeling emboldened by having been granted permission to continue her ministry, Nikki returned again to the donut shop the following week and then reported back to me on Sunday, proclaiming that things had taken a turn for the better that week. I asked what had happened, and she gave me a huge smile. "The pimps know I'm going to speak to them whether they like it or not, so they made me a deal. They agreed to give me ten minutes each week to speak, knowing that at least they'll get me to shut up after ten minutes." I congratulated her on her strategy and diligence, prayed for her, and she went happily along her way.

I didn't see her for a few weeks, then one Sunday she showed up again with another progress report. "Pastor, it's going so well. They invited me to one of their functions." After I admitted my total ignorance about the pimp world, she patiently explained it to me. "They invited me to speak to all of them at the pimp convention." That was a bit much for me; I giggled a bit before getting myself under control and asking what in the world a pimp convention was. All kinds of images were dancing in my head, but I wanted to hear firsthand what this event was.

Again displaying patience with her street-ignorant pastor, Nikki gave me the scoop. "Every year, they honor the Pimp of the Year in Hollywood. It's a big deal. They also honor the pimp who made the most money." Stuck in that sensitive place between cracking up and recoiling in horror, I asked, "But Nikki, tell me you're not going there. Nikki, you're not going there, are you?"

"Of course I'm going there!" she replied. "I'm going to minister to all those pimps."

After I stared incredulously at her for a couple of seconds, I again told her I would pray that the Lord would go with her because I sure wasn't about to.

Before the day of the big event, Nikki did her homework. She visited our men's home and asked a group of men gathered in the living room how many of them used to be pimps. More than a handful of arms were raised. Then she asked those guys if they would help her compose a gospel tract for pimps, using the language that pimps use on the street. Working together, they made a copy of a hundred dollar bill, because pimps like money, and on the back of it they crafted a message on how to receive forgiveness and new life in Christ, using pimp language. I don't remember it exactly, but it started out like, "Yo, player—if your Road Dog was knocking at the door of your momo, would you open up? Well, Jesus is knocking on the door of your heart, and He's the Ultimate Mac Daddy holding the keys to the track made of 'Bling Bling'—you need to let Him in."

It went on from there. I had only the vaguest idea what it meant, but it sure seemed like appropriate contextualization to me—the same approach they teach missionaries who are entering a foreign culture.

Nikki attended the convention. Prior to the event, she was waiting outside the building, where the pimps roll up in their fancy cars and make their grand entrance, not unlike the Academy Awards. So the guy who eventually won the coveted Pimp of the Year award arrived and got out of his limousine. As he walked down the red carpet into the building, he was strutting and displaying his fine clothes and massive ego, when all of a sudden it started raining hundred dollar bills on the red carpet. He's nodding away, thinking, *Of course they're distributing C-notes. I'm da man.* The assembled onlookers (mostly pimps and prostitutes who were not in the running for the big award) started grabbing the bills. As they looked at them, they realized the bills were fake. Then they saw the tract on the flip side, describing how God loved them and wanted to save them, even if they were pimps.

After a moment of confusion, the pimps started laughing. One of them ran over and showed the Pimp of the Year what was going on, and he laughed too. One of them yelled out, "That's got to be from that girl in the donut shop." They all had another good laugh and then somebody said, "She's cool," and another said, "We like her." One of the significant pimps—no, I have no idea how they rank these fellows—saw Nikki standing on the sidelines and said to her in front of everyone else, "Hey, baby, you're pretty cool, being a Christian and coming to our event. You just name it, we'll come to anything you want us to come to."

That was on Friday night. Saturday morning I received a phone call from Nikki. "Pastor, get ready, make sure you deliver a good message tomorrow." I always marvel at how people imply that we preachers decide whether to give a good or bad message on any given Sunday. I suppose if I had an ego about this, I'd wonder what makes them think any of our messages are anything but stellar. But ignoring the unintended putdown, I asked her why I needed to be on my game this particular weekend. Sounding a bit like Paul Revere, she explained, "The pimps are coming, the pimps are coming. They're coming to church tomorrow!" I admit I was baffled as to how to prepare for an entourage of pimps gracing our church.

Sure enough, upon taking the stage to kick off the service the next morning I looked up in the balcony and saw a whole row of pimps taking their seats. I've never seen so many purple and pink jackets in all my life. They stuck with us for the whole service. Toward the end of the service, I looked in the balcony as I gave the invitation for people to come forward to accept Christ. To my utter shock, I saw a group of pimps walk down the aisle and come to the front of the sanctuary, where I led them in a prayer to accept Christ as their Lord and Savior. I'll never forget one of the pimps asking Jesus to come into his life as one of the spotlights above the stage reflected off his gold grill.

Nikki taught me a thing or two about earning the right to be heard. She had endured ridicule and derision, but she loved those pimps into the Kingdom of God, right along with Jesus. And if you're wondering, a few of them did experience wholly transformed lives and were part of our church for a long time. They even helped us start our outreach to prostitutes. And it all happened because Nikki had earned the right to be heard. Her consistency won them over. If she had talked to them once or simply thrown the fake hundred dollar bills at them as a one-time effort, she would not have gotten anywhere. But she stuck with it, and God blessed her with amazing results because of her consistency and longevity. Some would call it longsuffering faithfulness. Whatever you want to call it, it's irreplaceable.

One of the people who lived on the block I visited every week in our Adopt-A-Block project was Jake. He was an old hippie who was pretty fed up with life. He rarely left his apartment. The first time I buzzed him on his building's intercom, it took him a long time to answer. When he did, I began to introduce myself, explaining I was there with my partner (Todd, who visited that block with me every week) to serve him and wondered if we could come up and meet him face-to-face. He listened for a few seconds and cut me off, yelling at me, layering lots of cuss words into his tirade against Christians, church people, pastors, do-gooders, and young adults (I'm probably twenty-five years his junior). Despite his obvious indifference, we returned week after week, and each week he'd cuss me out again, displaying so much hostility it was almost funny.

Finally, one week Jake gave in and said we could come up to meet him. I don't know if I wore him down or if it was some strategy to get rid of me once and for all, but we walked up to his unit, and he let us in his apartment. It was . . . trippy. He was a real hippie, had long, stringy hair, and was super skinny. His apartment was scantily furnished with very basic furniture. As far as I could tell, he spent most of his time messing around with his music system and a cheap keyboard setup. He seemed to be making some strange recordings for his own amusement, as if he were a radio DJ or maybe a lounge act. During that first visit two other unusual-looking fellows were on the couch and easy chairs in his living room. They were even less friendly than Jake.

Now that we were inside such a bizarre environment, we really didn't know what to say, so we just smiled and waited for him to talk. Eventually he said something about some bad experiences he'd had in church. I began to tell him about the Dream Center, and for some reason that really set him off. When he paused for a breath, I managed to ask if he'd play me some of his music. I praised his music and asked if he'd write us a song for next week. So we kept up the connection, built around his interest in music. He asked what kind of song I wanted him to write, and once he figured it out, he agreed to do so.

A few weeks later, sensing he was now comfortable with us, I invited him to come to our church. He kept refusing, for about a year or so. Then, to my surprise, one day I looked up from the pulpit and spotted him, this complete recluse, in the audience. And he came a few times after that. When it got close to Christmas, I asked what he planned to do on Christmas Eve. He said he had no plans, that he never did anything on Christmas Eve. I suggested that we go out that night to a movie, and he surprised me again by agreeing to the idea. He was really paranoid about leaving his apartment, but every once in a while he'd go somewhere with me.

So it took a couple of years, but Jake actually became a good friend. Later on, when I got married, he came to the wedding and actually sang at the reception. He was awful! Now, it didn't help that he followed our friend Lou Rawls, the incredible singer, who used to attend the Dream Center before he died. Of course, Jake thought he outsang Lou; he was really pleased with his own performance, and I was happy for him. We continued our friendship for years, until Jake finally moved away.

Now what was the purpose of all that? My cause is to help broken people heal. Jake didn't need clothes or food, but he really needed a friend. I could have beat a hasty retreat from his apartment the first day when he cussed me out over the intercom. I easily and rightly interpreted his words and demeanor to suggest that he wanted nothing to do with me. I doubt anybody would have faulted Todd and me for respecting his wishes and never returning to bug him again.

But I could sense that Jake had a need. I knew that my intentions were honorable—I wanted to love and serve him, for his own good—and genuinely believed that if he simply had a taste of that kindness, he'd appreciate it. I felt that what Todd and I were being exposed to was a facade. That he yelled at me and seemed so hostile was actually encouraging to me because I knew at least I represented a place to which he could divert his pain. How did I know he was struggling with pain? You don't cuss out complete strangers, especially those who express their desire to help you, unless something's awry in your life. His anger was as much a defense mechanism as anything.

By the way, earning the right to be heard isn't always pleasant. For months, each week when Todd and I visited Jake's apartment, not only was Jake less than cordial, but if his buddies were there, they would get verbally abusive. They would try anything they could think of to get under my skin. It was fascinating the way things unfolded. At first Jake just watched as his friends attacked. But after a few months, if they attacked, Jake would defend me! And I noticed that over time, he stopped using offensive language when we were there; he was treating us with greater and greater respect. Every once in a while I'd miss a week—if I had to preach at a church or conference out of town—and when I returned the next week he'd really let me have it. Although it was intense, I could tell that his attack reflected that our visits and friendship mattered to him.

The good that followed happened only because I had earned the right to be heard. I was outside my comfort zone—man, I couldn't even see my comfort zone from his place! It was a creepy environment, and we had nothing in common besides a need to be loved. And yet I knew this: whoever shows up the most in a person's life wins the battle for influence. So I kept showing up.

Not to dwell on Jake, but his story brings up another principle to keep in mind as you strive to carry out your cause: to have influence for your cause you may have to change the environment.

When Todd and I first began visiting Jake's apartment, the atmosphere was one of cynicism, mistrust, and disrespect. The place had a very weird vibe, with a heavy spirit to it. I always knew I had to spend a substantial amount of time in prayer before seeking out Jake. We could not have made any progress in a relationship with him if we had accepted that condition and tried to work within it. To change an environment you have to be so consistent in showing up and in the tenor of your work that the place becomes saturated with love. In other words, the kindness, love, and service simply force out any other conditions. You replace complaints with blessings. You focus on their needs rather than your interests.

A great example of changing the environment in order to fully love people comes from one of the couples who started serving in our Adopt-A-Block program. Soon after Emilio and Karina Cervantes began attending Angelus Temple, they started serving in the Dream Center's program. For their initial experience they went on one of our buses to a tough area of South Central Los Angeles. That area was centered around an old government housing project known as Pueblo del Rio, located next to the train tracks. The project has been a notorious gang site for more than forty years; the area is riddled with poverty and violence. Emilio loves to talk about their experiences at Pueblos:

> As soon as we got off the Dream Center bus, we felt the presence of God there. Right from the beginning we felt that God had something special in mind for that community. Pueblos has more than five hundred housing units in it. My wife and I went back to that place every Saturday, interacting with the people, taking care of them, and praying with them. God laid a burden on our hearts for that place and for those people.
>
> One day my wife and I were discussing how we each felt God moving us to start a small group for Pueblos that would meet every Wednesday night. There is such a big spiritual need there. We felt the small group would allow us to minister to people even more personally. So the Dream Center trained us in small-group leadership, and we began

the group. It's a real commitment for us because Pueblos is an hour and a half from our house. But we believed God wanted it and knew it could help the people.

When we started, no one would come to a small group on a Wednesday night in Pueblos. That's just how that place is. Many times we made that long drive and no one showed up. But we felt that God was pleased with our faithfulness, so we would return home, rejoicing and happy because we felt that it was pleasing God. We would go out there and just interact with families, and slowly the youth started to come, and then we were able to minister to some of the families. They started to open up to us.

We began taking the youth out of that place during our visits. For example, we'd take them to In-N-Out [a popular Southern California hamburger chain]. We've taken nineteen-year-old kids who were born and raised in the Pueblos neighborhood and found out they'd never been to an In-N-Out, they'd never been to a Starbucks. There aren't any of those kinds of places in the Pueblos area, so we have to drive a long time to get to them. Even if we take the youth to a movie theater, it's a thirty-five-minute drive outside of South Central.

So we had more and more opportunities to bless the kids and their families. My wife and I began talking about how to adjust our family finances—you know, cutting back on spending and expenses—so we'd have more money to sow into the lives of these kids in Pueblos. We wanted them to have more opportunities. We had seen that when we took them out of that environment, even just by going to a burger place or a theater, those were the times they would open up to us and we were able to minister God's love and God's Word. It was very special because they trusted us enough to open their hearts. Many of them shared things with us that they had never told anyone in their lives.

We were praying that God would help us have more seed to sow into the lives of these people. One night, I talked to a young man who was a drug dealer who lived in the neighborhood. He came to the small group. I asked him what the biggest need was in Pueblos because I was trying to figure out what kind of help would matter the most. This young man looked at me and my wife and said, "The biggest need here in Pueblos is love and hope. We don't have those two things. Society has forgotten about this place. The politicians, the school board, the city of LA, the police department—they don't pay attention to us. We desperately need love and hope." I looked him in the eye and told him that Jesus had not forgotten about this place. But that young man's words got to me.

Several months passed by, and on Thanksgiving weekend I was at home, thanking God for His blessings and meditating in God. And I had an impression in my heart that God spoke to me and said, "Emilio, do you know the biggest blessing a person could receive from Me?" I wasn't even going to try to answer that! The Lord put the answer in my heart: "The biggest blessing is having the freedom to give it all away." I stored that away in my heart.

Meanwhile, at Pueblos we were gaining greater favor with the people because we were there every week, on Wednesdays and Saturdays. We were going into people's homes and literally coming out with trash cans full of witchcraft items. One of those nights I felt the Lord speak to my heart again and tell me that if a person is willing to give it all away, they'll have such freedom that nothing can stop them. That led my wife and me to start asking God even more fervently for that kind of freedom. We knew He could change that place and do amazing things. We kept asking Him for more seed to sow and to give away, to bless those people.

Then we heard a sermon about extraordinary grace and extraordinary favor and about believing God for an extraordinary year. My wife and I told God that we believed that the coming year would be one of great blessing and that we would be able to have a big soul-winning event in Pueblos and that He would do amazing things.

The next day, Emilio received a call from an executive of his employer's biggest competitor. He wanted to recruit Emilio to work for them. Emilio agreed to meet with the competitor. Prior to that meeting, he prayed long and hard about what to do. He received a sense from God of a specific deal he should seek. He went into that conversation resolved not to settle for anything less. The competitor kept negotiating with Emilio, making him four outstanding offers that far exceeded what he was currently making. But each offer was shy of what Emilio believed the Lord had set as the standard. After the fourth offer, the executive requested the check from the waitress, paid the bill at the register, and walked out to the parking lot with Emilio. When they reached their cars and prepared to depart with no deal in place, Emilio played his trump card:

I said to him, "Do you know why I'm fighting so hard for that extra $800 a month? Because that money will go a long way for the kids in Pueblos. It's $10,000 a year. That may not seem like a lot to you, but it could make a big difference in Pueblos." And right after that he agreed to the deal. The deal that we struck more than doubled my pay. But I wasn't doing it for me. I was fighting for the blessing of Pueblos. I knew that the raise was how God was providing the seed we asked for. He had spoken to my heart about what to ask for in the negotiations after ten days of praying. No matter what that man said during our negotiations, I knew that he was going to give me that amount.

Right after that I felt that God was speaking to me again. He said, *I want you to put on the biggest outreach event that Pueblos has ever seen. And I want you and your wife to give $25,000 for that event.* Realize that we're in a recession, and that money's coming from a working guy and a stay-at-home mom. You know, $25,000 for us is huge; that's a big number, and a huge step of faith. But that was God's plan, and we did it.

The event took place. About one thousand people showed up; nothing remotely close to such an event had ever been held in Pueblos. There was live music, carnival games, and all kinds of giveaways of clothing, toys, and food. To this day people in that community talk about the event. It has gone a long way toward changing the environment and enabling Pueblos's residents to adopt a different perspective on life—a perspective of love and hope.

Emilio and Karina are reveling in the expanded opportunities they now have for ministry with the people of Pueblos. They are determined to seek further blessings from God for a resource center for teenagers. That facility would also give them a regular place for their small group meeting. Currently they meet outdoors on a street corner; hopefully they will be meeting indoors before long.

Emilio and his wife had a big dream but started small—they met with the Pueblos people regularly and eventually started a small group. They didn't spend gobs of time talking about strategies and options; they solved the needs they witnessed by faithfully returning to that desolate place week after week, regardless of how many people (if any) showed up to meet with them. Their diligence impressed the locals and earned them the right to be heard—and to hear what was on people's hearts.

The residents accept them as people who belong to the Pueblos community, an honor they have earned through the power of their consistent presence and their unfailing interest in serving. And their love and faithfulness to the people, their trust in God, and their excitement about being free to give away what God gave them have birthed a new atmosphere in Pueblos. No, it's not Rodeo Drive in Beverly Hills, but it's not the same dangerous, hopeless place it was two years ago, either.

Emilio and Karina had paid for everything in secret and managed to keep it a secret for seven months—until I spilled the beans during one of our services. They were embarrassed that I told everyone they paid for the event because they simply wanted all the glory to go to God. They will be the first to tell you that the payback for them is the joy of seeing lives changed in that run-down, forgotten part of Los Angeles and knowing that God found a way to use them in that transformation process.

What a beautiful example of how to pursue your cause! You don't do it for public recognition or private gain. You don't do it because you believe you will get more rewards from God—more "jewels in your crown." You do it because God wants to use you in that way and because you will experience the pure pleasure of serving Him by loving people. It doesn't get any better than that.

WHAT I'VE LEARNED

- God's vision for your life is huge, but you accomplish it through a series of tiny steps.
- Influence is achieved by affecting one life at a time.
- Don't spend your precious time debating the fine points of the cause; identify the core need, address the need, then discuss the situation once you've blessed those in need.

- You are not likely to make a difference unless you feel urgency about the need that must be addressed.
- Earn the right to be heard through consistency and longevity.
- You may have to change the atmosphere of the place to which you've been called.
- Every little thing you do matters; there is no wasted effort in God's Kingdom.

CHAPTER 9

BUILD YOUR TEAM TO CHANGE THE WORLD

ONE OF THE GREAT IRONIES in our culture is that leaders receive the credit for the amazing things that happen during their watch. I don't want to diminish the importance of what great leaders do or the necessity of effective leadership, but I am always puzzled when we reward leaders and ignore their teammates. Great leaders admit they could not have accomplished what gets credited to them without the help of a lot of people who worked hard alongside them and behind the scenes. In fact, the Dream Center reaches 30,000 people every week. There's no way we could do that without the contributions of our hundreds of staff and volunteers—not to mention the 8,000 or so people who visit for a week each year for a short-term (or as I call it, turbo-charged) missions trip.

Fulfilling your cause will almost certainly require you to work in cooperation with many other people. Most of them will be role-players—people who work with you for a brief time and provide some type of minor, specialized service. But had they not been present to add the value they did, your story would be different. Sometimes you'll be blessed with one or more people who play a more significant role in the pursuit of your cause. Either way, those colleagues are partners who help bring your cause to life.

Partnership is a critical element in the pursuit of your dream. At the Dream Center, I have been fortified by three kinds of partners: temporary helpers, long-term partners, and God. Each of those, in their own way, is indispensable. You gain the greatest leverage from their involvement if you recognize that you cannot accomplish your dream solo; you must welcome and appreciate the assistance of value-adding partners.

The greatest partner I've had at the Dream Center has been my father. From day one, he not only opened the door for my opportunity at Bethel Temple, which transitioned into the remarkable journey at the Dream Center, but he has labored alongside me every step of the way. In addition to leading his huge church in Phoenix, he has logged tens of thousands of miles flying and driving back and forth to Los Angeles to help me do everything imaginable for these first sixteen years. He has tallied untold hours doing every conceivable task for this cause, from preaching and dispensing resources to raising money and endlessly praying. He embraced this as an extension of his cause and has done whatever was needed to keep things moving.

He has been a tireless encourager and supporter. Think about this: when he was sixty years old, he knew the Dream Center desperately needed money, so he contacted everyone he knew, including the people in his congregation, and said he was going to run from Phoenix to Los Angeles to help us raise money. He asked all those contacts to pledge a certain amount of money for every mile he completed on his trek through the desert.

My dad is not a marathoner. He simply wanted to come up with a creative, attention-grabbing way of getting people to support what we were doing. So there he was, at age sixty, running through the desert toward Los Angeles, covering nearly four hundred miles in about three weeks' time. I ran beside him for about ten miles, and then he just kept going. If you average it out, he essentially ran a marathon each day of the journey. It took a real toll on him physically. His feet swelled several sizes. He contracted phlebitis in his legs. In fact, he never mentions it, but he still is plagued by some of the aftereffects today. He could have stopped at any time en route and nobody would have thought less of him. But he was wholly committed to providing any kind of help he could. When he finally chugged his way down Hollywood Boulevard, he was thrilled that his feat—and his feet—had raised nearly a million dollars for us through that crazy act of love and support.

For years my dad has given every honorarium he receives from speaking at churches and conferences to the Dream Center. He speaks often at our church, our chapel, and our program graduations. I know he is proud of me, but even more so, he is proud of what I have allowed God to do through me on the way to seeing God's vision become a reality.

What makes my father such a great partner is that he doesn't want credit for what he has done. We've been on numerous television programs together, and it's common for us to keep trying to lift the other up as the one who deserves the attention. I'll call him the real pastor of our church, and he'll return the compliment. He'll talk about my perseverance until I interrupt and tell stories about his amazing support. Our relationship has shown me that the old truism is accurate: it is incredible how much can be accomplished when you don't care who gets the credit. And he is a double threat as a partner: he'll do whatever is necessary to advance the cause, and he refuses to quit. You cannot ask for more than that.

The glue that binds partners together is their mutual passion for the cause.

The glue that binds partners together is their mutual passion for the cause. When the cause is central, the nature of one's title or tasks loses its meaning. It's all about doing what God has called you to do and letting Him take care of the results while you enjoy the ride. If you can envision your cause as a relay race, you expect to hand off the baton to others who will complete legs of the journey that you cannot or should not run. That greatly benefits the cause: after all, it's the team, not an individual member of the team, that wins. Ultimate influence is not achieved by starting strong, but by finishing strong. You'll need good partners to help you do that.

As I have disclosed throughout this book, I was in way over my head early in my time in Los Angeles. I had all kinds of ideas about how to do my ministry but little idea about how to do God's ministry. Fortunately, my dad was helping me out from a distance.

Before heading for Los Angeles, I attended Grand Canyon University in Arizona. While there, I had a brief encounter with Aaron Jayne, another student on campus. He was heavily into alcohol and drugs while he was in college, although I did not know him well enough to be aware of that. One day I invited him to attend a Christmas event at my dad's church. Aaron remembers that adventure:

> I decided to go to the big Christmas show. I wasn't a Christian. My dad was a preacher, but he abandoned my family when I was young. That was my only image of God, so I hated

Christians for years. But I had nothing else going on, so I went to the church's event. True to my lifestyle at that time, I dropped some acid beforehand. I figured that would really make the show special because it was supposed to feature lasers and flying angels. While I was at the church, I sensed there was something different about it, in a positive way, but at that time in my life I wasn't looking to be a Christian.

Some time went by during that Christmas season. I was sleeping in my car back then because I had nowhere else to go. I became depressed and suicidal. Without any other real options, I returned to that big church that had the Christmas event, and I got radically saved. I went back week after week. One Sunday I was talking to Matthew's dad on my way out the back door after a service. I was still in college, but I told his dad I didn't know what to do with my life. And Pastor Tommy said, "Well, why don't you go to Los Angeles and help my son?"

So I dropped out of college and drove to Los Angeles. When I first got there, the two guys who were helping Pastor Matthew run the place sized me up and didn't think I was going to make it. The outreach ministry was just getting off the ground, and they didn't have a place for me, so I was sleeping in a hallway—I didn't even have a room—and I kept all my clothes in the trunk of my car. It wasn't much of a step up in some ways, but I really felt I didn't have anything else to do with my life. I had been at college on a scholarship but didn't want to go back there. I could have switched colleges to study for the ministry, but I didn't have the money to go to Bible college. Actually, I didn't have the money to do much of anything. But at the Dream Center there was a vision that was so big it was attractive. And I figured there wasn't much in life that I could do, but I knew I could serve.

Soon after I arrived in Los Angeles, Thanksgiving came. We fed six thousand people in the church parking lot. I spent the day washing dishes. We had no hot water, so we had to keep boiling water, one pot at a time, and it took us about eight hours to do dishes for six thousand people. But it was really all about the dream. Matthew had a dream that was so huge I was ready to give my entire life to the dream. Whatever it took, it didn't matter. Wherever I lived, it didn't matter. Whatever I ate, it didn't matter. It was all about the dream.

I was a volunteer at the Dream Center for about nine years. During that time I moved from place to place on the grounds; I lived in about twelve different rooms over that time. I had no regular income, but the Dream Center took care of me. As a volunteer I did not get a salary or wages, but they paid my auto insurance, which I couldn't afford. All of my meals were provided at the Dream Center, and I was living rent free, so I really didn't need a whole lot of money. Every month my mom would send me maybe a hundred dollars or so, or there would be somebody visiting the Dream Center who I'd drive around for two or three days, and when I'd drop them off at the airport, they'd give me a little bit of money. That's literally how I lived for those nine years. I probably lived on a hundred to two hundred dollars a month. And every month God provided what I needed through Pastor Matthew and different people. It never felt like a struggle to me. I never felt like I was in need. I was too focused on the cause to worry about those things.

One of the things I've learned about great partners like Aaron is that they are low maintenance. They do not put a lot of personal demands on you because they are just as passionate about the cause as you are. You know you can trust them with any resource and under any circumstance. They may have different gifts than you have—hopefully that's true, so they can cover dimensions of the work that you are not skilled to handle—but they have the same interest and commitment. They are not worried about their retirement fund or position; they are fully invested in the cause. Aaron eventually became a full-time, paid staff person, but it was not at his urging; it was our decision to do that to free him up to take on other tasks we wanted him to do. He chose to continue to live on campus until he got married a few years ago. He recalls:

> Once I got involved serving people and loving people through the Dream Center, I knew this was my life's calling. I didn't really know how God was going to provide for me when I was forty years old, and I didn't have any idea what my life might look like then. And honestly, I didn't care. You read all these amazing stories of people in the ministry from years and years ago, and no one was ever in it because they wanted to be wealthy or famous and provided for.
>
> When I headed out to Los Angeles, I looked at this adventure as an opportunity to be a missionary. Once I got a taste of it, I was prepared to be a missionary for the rest of my life if that's what God called me to. That may have been just because I was young, and when you're young, you don't really think about the future. But I was probably about twenty-eight before I went on salary, and even then the only reason I went on salary was because they came to me and said they were going to do it; I didn't ask for it or expect it. Like everything else on this journey, I just accepted it. I knew I was going to be serving and loving people, which was my calling. I expected to be at the Dream Center, still serving, because it was the kind of mission that brought me there in the first place.

One thing that helped me wrap my mind around my role in all of this was a sermon that Pastor Matthew preached on being addicted to the ministry. He talked about some of the disciples who worked with Paul, and he described them as men who became addicted to the ministry. I can totally relate to that, especially with my background. You become an addict by taking that first hit. Then you take another hit and another hit, and before you know it, you're addicted. Once you're addicted, nothing else really matters. We have been working with addicts in Los Angeles for years, and you see that nothing besides their fix matters to them. Addicts don't care if they live in a cardboard box in an alley; they don't care what people think of them; they don't pay attention to how they look. Addicts will do whatever it takes to get their next hit. I've seen addicts sell their children to drug dealers in exchange for crack—because addicts will do whatever it takes to get that next hit. That's what our cause is like, an addiction. I am obsessed with it.

One night we were sitting around in Pastor Matthew's apartment downtown—this was before either of us got married—and we were watching ESPN. It was about ten o'clock at night. All of a sudden he just jumped up and said, "We gotta go serve somebody." I was like, "What?" And he repeated, "We gotta go serve somebody." So we jumped in his car at ten at night and drove around. We found a homeless person, picked him up, and took him to Denny's. That was a lesson to us that when you're an addict and you've got to have that next hit, there's nothing you can do to stop that feeling or replace that need. I think it's that way with whatever your cause is. You get addicted to it, and you do whatever it takes to satisfy that craving to serve.

It hasn't always been a smooth ride. In the beginning I

had to overcome fear. When you grow up in a small town in Texas, like I did, Los Angeles is a very scary place. When I moved into this area there were a number of people who got shot on the streets outside my window. One day even I got shot at. I've had my windows busted and my tires slashed. I'm not playing the martyr card; I've never felt like a martyr or like someone who deserves special treatment because of what I do or the kind of people we try to help. All I'm saying is that we've been through some tough stuff and that reality played on my preexisting fears of the big city. I didn't want to go out into the tough sections of LA when I started out.

In those first days I talked to Matthew about it, and he said, "You know, 'perfect love casts out fear.'[14] If you'll fall in love with the people and this city, you won't be afraid of it." I didn't have a better plan, and I really respected him, so I took his advice and began to fall in love with the people and the city. Soon I found I wasn't afraid of it anymore.

In doing so, I also learned that working at having a ministry doesn't really allow you to fall in love with people like building relationships does. You can get so caught up in developing your ministry that people just become accessories in the process. We stopped trying to reach the entire city of Los Angeles and instead focused on reaching deep into a couple of blocks in front of the Dream Center. We visited those same blocks every single week, knocked on the same doors every week, and saw the same faces and talked to the same people. As we built those relationships, we began to know those residents and fall in love with them, and we began to know what their needs were. For me, practically speaking, that was how I fell in love with people. I got to know them and see what they struggled with, like when I saw an entire family in a one-room apartment with a single mattress on the floor. That'll break your heart and move you with compassion, and then miracles begin to occur if you allow them to. Pastor taught us to see that.

I've heard many leaders describe effective partnerships that are initiated and maintained on the basis of strong interpersonal chemistry—you like each other, so you work together. That kind of chemistry is helpful. But in my experience there is no substitute for developing a partnership based on people's excitement about the vision. You can put up with someone who will never be your best friend—or even someone you'd never voluntarily hang out with during your free time—as long as you are both sold out to the same vision. You can be good friends and have lots of fun with someone without accomplishing anything of value; but when you are yoked up with one or more people who share your vision, you'll produce great things together, even if you never become best buddies. The best of all situations, of course, is when you have a deep friendship with someone who shares the vision—the kind of partner relationship I've had with Aaron.

God has blessed me over the years with a multitude of great partners. Those relationships can be thought of as divine partnerships. When Aaron arrived in Los Angeles and pulled his car into the church parking lot, I had no reason to expect him to be a lifelong colleague in some of the most stressful, dangerous ministry ventures you can imagine. He did not arrive with special training, a wealth of experience, impressive recommendations, or a great plan for the future. But he was the first guy I met who was willing to totally sell out for the vision from day one. No matter what has happened—and he has been through some rough situations during his tenure with us—his commitment never changed. In these past sixteen years, the Lord has brought us many people who have had a solid and enduring commitment to our vision. And that is precisely why the Dream

Center has been successful: not because of me, but because of the tremendous partnerships that have been forged in the heat of hardship and vision. Like all groups that exist to fulfill a God-given vision, the results depend upon the strength of the team that is committed to fulfilling the vision.

People like Aaron, Todd, Caroline, Emilio, Alena—people you've read about so far and hundreds more just like them—are the kind of partners you want to surround yourself with. These are the kind of people who are more interested in pleasing God by loving people than in saving up for a retirement villa on the French Riviera or generating media coverage over their heroic exploits among the poor. These are the people God uses to change the world, in whatever way He has called them to serve. And it's about accepting that each of these precious colleagues will build up influence and impact in ways and in places that I will never touch. I am thrilled about that because the dream is not to promote Matthew Barnett; it is to do the work that God carved out for us to take on together. In a great team, everyone plays a critical role; the team cannot survive without each person bringing his or her unique contribution to the table.

Who are your partners in the pursuit of your cause? How well do you support them and thank God for their involvement?

Developing great human partnerships is one aspect of your cause. Developing a great partnership with God is another.

Keep things in perspective. Your cause is a gift from God, specially designed with you in mind. Not only does He want you to succeed in championing that cause, He wants to be part of it. If truth be told, when your cause becomes bigger than your relationship with God, you're on the highway to failure.

Even though this is a book about pursuing your God-given cause and making the most of the privilege, I would be remiss if I did not share some thoughts and experiences regarding your relationship with God. He created you in order to have a loving relationship with you. He sent His son, Jesus Christ, to die an ugly, painful, and unjust death so that your relationship with Him could continue and grow. And the purpose of your life is to enjoy your relationship with Him and to obey His calling for your life, which is all about serving Him by serving other people.

In the course of developing your connection with God, prayer is perhaps your most important tool. Prayer can be a strange thing. For me, it was simply a source of bondage and frustration for many years. I never saw prayer as having anything to do with maintaining a relationship with God; I saw it as something that I had to do in order to win over God and impress Him enough to get Him to bless my efforts. I used to get nothing out of my prayer life; it's embarrassing to admit it now, but prayer was often an attempt to get God to bless me because I took time from my busy life to talk to Him. Prayer was just a means to an end, a way for me to manipulate Him to give me what I wanted.

Because of that warped view of prayer, I was always watching the clock whenever I'd pray. I believed that the longer I prayed, the more spiritual I was, and therefore the more God owed me. It was a foolish point of view built on the notion of a conditional relationship, as if God were looking down saying, "Wow, I'm going to bless you more because you prayed forty-five minutes instead of just thirty."

One day I realized that I didn't need to manipulate God to get behind my ministry because He was actually in front of it, leading the way and fully involved in it. After all, He originally gave it to me; He already loves it. So at that moment I changed both my understanding and practice of prayer.

These days my commitment is to have some prayer time in the morning, between six and nine, starting whenever I felt ready to pray. Then I pray until I feel full. That allows me to pray off and on as I'm moving about, whether I'm walking the halls of the Dream Center, or in my office meditating, or driving my car. Every morning I ask God to give me the right spirit in every encounter with people throughout the day.

Over time I learned that prayer is not an obligation undertaken to make God happy; it is something that I need to constantly be in fellowship with Him, regardless of the amount of time it consumes or the place where it happens. It may be three to four minutes here, a few more minutes there, maybe another five minutes in between two activities. When I'm in the car alone, I generally keep the radio off, giving me a few more uninterrupted minutes to seek God. If I'm walking across campus from one meeting to another, I'll take the time to listen to God. Sometimes I run a few laps around the church building, and that's another great time to connect with Him. Even some days when I take my kids to a nearby park and watch them play, I can spend wonderful time alone with God while watching my children and encouraging them.

> **Every morning I ask God to give me the right spirit in every encounter with people throughout the day.**

For years, I thought such an approach was wrong—maybe even blasphemous. After all, you have to be in a secluded, quiet place to pray, don't you? Sadly, my relationship with God suffered because of all the rules and limitations that colored my view of prayer and my understanding of what a relationship with God is all about. Once I realized that God is portable, flexible, and that He is in the ordinary circumstances and everyday occurrences of my life, having a dynamic relationship with Him became much easier—and a whole lot more fun and practical.

It's also very personal because my prayer time is now based on relationship. It envelops every aspect of my life and all matters of the heart and soul. If I hadn't learned to see prayer as more than just a strategy to get His blessing on my work and learned to incorporate prayer into a real relationship, there's no way the Dream Center would exist today and no way that I would still be involved in significant service.

Sometimes I will enter into God's presence and I won't say a word. I used to think I had to talk all the time when I was with God. Now, it's more like a flesh-and-blood relationship. Some days I'm chatty and full of things to tell Him; other days I say nothing the whole time. Sometimes my conversation with God is energetic and animated; other times I'll just sit and meditate. It reminds me of times with my dad. Without question, we love each other. Sometimes we'll drive someplace and the two of us will talk nonstop; other days we might drive an hour without saying anything. Either way I'm still comforted because I'm in his presence.

That's what your relationship with God can be like too. If you miss a day or two, He is not going to reach down from heaven with a paddle to smack you over the head and say, "Boy, you missed two days." Like any close friend, God simply picks up where the two of you left off.

God knows you better than anyone does—even better than you know yourself. When it comes to prayer, He communicates with different people in different ways—in ways that are most comfortable or plausible for them. God communicates with me through distractions and impressions. Does that sound weird? He may have a different approach with you. But for me, it works. Whenever I become extremely distracted from my cause, it's like a sign that it's time for me to pay attention to Him and carve out some time alone with Him. That's the trigger He uses to get my attention—distractions from the thing that consumes me.

Once I realize it's one of those times, I do whatever I need to do to withdraw for a while. I close my eyes, invite Him to speak to me, and simply listen. If I have a chance to go home, I go to my bedroom, shut the door, and just lie on the bed and wait to hear from Him. If I cannot be home, I have developed a few other getaway spots too. And when I go through a prolonged period when things seem consistently distracting or confusing, then I know I need to leave town for a day or two to listen. There is a place in the mountains nearby where I can go. And as a regular practice I will go there once a month. I might drive my car up there, park overlooking the city, and just wait. There is no schedule or clock involved. I've been there for less than an hour, and I've been there for four hours, receiving impressions from God.

God usually gets my attention by bringing to mind things that are not in line with the cause: stupid attitudes, little annoyances, indefensible offenses, wrong ideals, character shifts—whatever it might be. God provides very clear and vivid impressions, leaving no doubt in my mind about what I need to do.

Realize that He speaks to people differently. Some people hear a voice. Others receive signs. Some are led to Scripture verses. The means is not as important as your commitment to making the time to listen when He is ready to speak to you. If you are serious about pursuing the cause He has given you, prayer is a crucial component of that effort because you must allow God to lead you. Even if you have great mentors helping you to mature, chances are good that there will be situations when you are being asked to do something that your mentors have not done. Yet, unwilling to set you up for failure, God will give you the exact guidance you need for such moments—but you need to be in touch with Him and be able to absorb His wisdom.

How can you follow God's leading as you pursue your cause? Here are a few suggestions based on what many of us do around the Dream Center:

- Understand God's principles in relation to your cause. When we speak to groups about what God has done through the Dream Center, we do not talk about our methods because the impact we have had is not related to our methods. Besides, what good would it do for us to share our methods for how to reach Los Angeles if you're not in Los Angeles? It's all about principles. If you're around the Dream Center for long, you'll hear someone say something like, "Find a need and fill it," "Whatever you want in life, give it away," or, "You don't have to look far to see a need—they're everywhere." Statements like these aren't catchy slogans to us; every time we repeat them,

Find a need and fill it.

they reinforce our vision. The underlying principles are central to our influence, and your own principles will be central to yours as well—no matter what your cause is or where you're located.

- When you speak about your cause and the progress being made in relation to the cause, get in the habit of giving God the credit. You don't have to be obnoxious about it, but consistently recognizing the source of your power and positive results is an important element in waking others up to the fact that a cause-driven life is fueled by God, not human talent and ingenuity. Besides, words that glorify God are pleasing to Him.

- Do not force your schedule onto your cause. Allow God's timing to prevail. Our tendency is to rush and get it done quickly; God's tendency is to allow us to grow through engagement in the process and to enjoy the unexpected elements of the journey. As my father taught me, "Delay is not denial." Don't get frustrated if everything doesn't stay on schedule. We have often found it is God's way of protecting us from things of which we were not aware.

- Pray constantly with open ears. Act on what you hear. Give thanks whenever you can.

- Take risks that you believe God will bless. There is nothing worse than a ministry that plays it safe! As you read through the Bible, and the Old Testament in particular, you will find God asking His servants to take outrageous risks—and then protecting them and propelling them to unbelievable victories to show His power and to reward their faith. God does not play the game the same way we do. But He is an unparalleled partner. Let Him play His role; your role is simply to follow Him with confidence and consistency.

Just as a solid marriage is based on a husband and wife's fully trusting each other, a genuine partnership with God is based on complete trust as well.

Six years ago we were blessed by the arrival of Sandy and Craig Kinart. They had been members of my father's church in Phoenix and were active in the street ministry there. Now they are full-time leaders in our work, serving as houseparents in the men's discipleship program and overseeing the clothing distribution ministry. They originally came to us, kind of on loan, to help out during the Katrina influx. After spending a few weeks helping out, they felt that this was where they were meant to be. But their involvement in the Dream Center has been orchestrated through their partnership with God in the pursuit of their cause. Sandy marvels at how God has worked in their lives:

> A little bit before we came here, God had placed on our hearts that we should quit our jobs, sell our home, and get

into full-time ministry. That seemed like a big step, so I did a twenty-one-day fast. I didn't tell anybody except Craig. And God said, "Simplify your life." I wondered how much simpler our life could get. At that time we were bringing homeless people into our home to live with us. And then things began to get more clear. Instead of having garage sales, I started giving everything away. After that it was, "I really want you guys to trust Me. I want you to quit your jobs."

I said I felt that God was moving us to sell our house and live on-site so we could be in the midst of the work. So we went around about it, with Craig suggesting I do that but adding that he'd keep his job just in case. Meanwhile, I went ahead and quit my job. And then the Lord moved Craig, and he said, "You're right, and let's sell the house, too. I saw you following God's direction, and I was feeling left out. And God said to me that the only person stopping me was me. So I quit my job."

Some of our friends were really worried about this. They said we should rent out our house, just in case this didn't work out. I said, "What do you mean? If we want to trust God, failure's not an option. And if we sell everything and walk away and do what He's calling us to do, it's His responsibility to take care of us. And as long as we're walking in integrity and doing what we're supposed to be doing, we don't have to worry about that."

So we haven't worried. We probably have less materially than we've ever had in our lives. I'm in my fifties, but this is the most fulfilled time I've ever had in my life. My kids don't understand it—they think we're nuts—but this is where God wants us, and He has taken care of us every step of the way. We've been here almost six years now, and we love what we're doing. But one thing is for sure: we could not do this if we weren't empowered by the Holy Spirit. He directs us and leads us. He gives us discernment and wisdom in the decisions we make, and that's critical because we make some life-or-death decisions in our work here. So we have to always be sure that our relationship with God is good. Without that, we'd be sunk.

Your team will consist of two kinds of partners: other people who embrace the same cause as you, and the God who gave you the cause in the first place. A team that lacks either of those partners is a team that's not yet ready to play ball.

WHAT I'VE LEARNED

- If you can accomplish your dream without partnerships, your dream is not big enough.
- If your cause is bigger than your relationship with God, you won't reach the cause's full potential.
- When it doesn't matter who gets the credit, you and your team can accomplish amazing things.
- God's timing is the right timing; don't get hung up on your schedule.
- Your investment in your relationship with God is the best investment you can make in the pursuit of your cause.

CHAPTER 10

THE RIGHT TIME TO QUIT

Do you know the most common two-word expression you will probably use as you pursue the cause within you?

I quit.

A few years ago the Dream Center hosted a fund-raiser in which I was shooting free throws in our gym. Like my dad's run across the desert, people pledged a certain amount of money based on the number of free throws I made within a twenty-four-hour period. I love basketball and used to play competitively, so this figured to be an enjoyable as well as profitable adventure.

I shot free throw after free throw for hours. By the time I'd shot more than five thousand free throws, my wrist and right shoulder gave out. The human body simply is not meant for that kind of excessive wear, but I was determined to keep shooting as long as there was time left on the clock. I had about six hours left—that represented potentially thousands of dollars for the Dream Center, so I refused to quit.

THE CAUSE WITHIN YOU

Watching me from afar, one of our donors thought I was just tired and was going to give up early. He didn't know about my injuries and the pain I was in; he wanted to encourage me to keep going, so he called me from his cell phone. I took a brief break to answer the phone and heard him say the magic words: "Pastor, I'm upping the ante. From this point on, every free throw you make is worth $500." I clarified what I thought he had said, thanked him profusely, hung up, and started to cry.

At that point I was unable to lift my arm, and my wrist was swollen and throbbing. After hitting more than five thousand shots, I don't think anyone would have thought less of me for calling it quits. Besides, if they failed to show adequate concern I could always get one of those wrist casts and a shoulder harness to really wring the sympathy vote and save face!

But in the midst of my instant pity party, I started thinking about the stakes: $500 for each successful shot! Man, I could be at NBA pay level in a few hours—if I could just lift my arm and move my wrist. I stood there begging God to do something. I knew I couldn't continue the way I was.

A minute later, while explaining to God why I could not take advantage of that moment, He impressed upon me that wimping out was not an option. A donor was stepping up to provide the support I'd been praying for; this was no time for me to end the contest. Courage and continuity is great, but I was in growing agony. So I told God that if He was so intent upon my continuing, this battle was no longer about me; it was now up to Him to work it out somehow. I reminded Him—as if He needed the memory jog—that I was doing this for the sake of the people He loved and had called me to serve, the people I've grown to love. "If You want this, Lord, You touch my body and make this happen."

I boldly returned to the free-throw line, fully expecting a miracle. After dribbling the ball a couple of times, I lined up my shot and

162

winged it toward the basket. The moment the ball left my hand, wobbling off the edge of the backboard, a couple of feet to the right of the rim, a blizzard of pain coursed through the right side of my body and lit up my brain. I was on fire inside. I probably let out a scream of pain, I don't know; I was suddenly transported to another world, a world of torture and agony.

Despite all the lofty truths we have considered regarding the blessing of being a blessing, the hard reality is that living for your cause is very difficult work. Sometimes it provides over-the-top pleasure; other times it will be excruciatingly painful. Making an impact demands perseverance, and that is what makes quitting so attractive at times. You simply get to a stage in the journey where you have had enough, for any number of reasons, and are ready to call it a game.

Have I ever felt like quitting? I don't have enough fingers and toes to count the times. My dad's reaction to such moments of weakness has been helpful: "It's okay to think about quitting. It's not okay to quit." Having thought about quitting without actually following through, I can certainly tell you it is worth sticking it out to pursue the full potential of your cause—but sometimes it's a bear to do so.

> **Have I ever felt like quitting? I don't have enough fingers and toes to count the times.**

There seem to be two types of situations that move us to feel like giving up. The first are tasks we engage in that are important for the continuation of the cause. The second are situations that lead us to the brink of leaving the cause altogether. Let's explore these separately.

When I was growing up, my parents had all kinds of expressions to shape our thinking about our choices and behavior. One of those that seemed so silly was, "Quitters never win, and winners never quit." It just sounds so simplistic and childish. But the biggest problem with that saying is that it's true.

Along the way to pursuing your cause, you will encounter more than a few of those days. You know what I mean by "those days," don't you? Those days when everything seems to go wrong; when all of your colleagues let you down; when the people you're trying to serve show you utter disregard and contempt; when you're physically run-down and don't have the energy to keep slugging it out; when one little screwup snowballs into a gigantic problem; when a simple resource that would facilitate an enormous breakthrough is missing; when someone important misinterprets you and cancels out days of hard and delicate work already completed because of it. When those days pop up, you can't even remember why you thought this cause was such a great idea in the first place. I've had my share of those days.

When those days strike, you need to step back, take a deep breath, and relax. Giving up doesn't solve the problem. It's all just part of the testing we go through that prepares us for—or disqualifies us from—bigger challenges and breakthroughs that are on the horizon. Remember, you are pursuing the cause within you as part of a team. During those moments, call upon your team to muster the resources you need to maintain forward movement. Your ultimate teammate, God, will surely have the answer you need—maybe not the one you want, but the one you need.

To be honest, as I stood at the free-throw line the night of the fund-raiser, pain shooting through my arm and wrist even after praying for relief, I was pretty ticked off at God. I felt like I was throwing medical caution to the wind, I was stepping up to do my share—but where was He? With more than a trace of determination—and anger—I told Him that I intended to keep on shooting, and whatever happened was up to Him. I tried to toss another ball into the hoop and flames of pain surged through my body.

I was really upset now—and I was not going to give in. So I tried some creative approaches. I took a few feeble shots left-handed. I tried drop kicking the ball into the net. I tried punching it in with my left hand. Remembering my soccer training, I even tried to head a few balls through the iron hoop.

And then the most amazing thing happened. I grabbed a ball and tried shooting with my right hand again. It was less painful than before. I tried another; it was less painful than the previous shot. Again and again I tossed the ball toward the hoop, flicking the ball in a high arc toward the basket, bending my swollen wrist—but now without pain. The shots started dropping in. Dazed, I hurriedly grabbed the remaining balls off the rack, one after another, and tossed them toward the rim. *Swish! Swish! Swish!* Where were the NBA scouts when I needed them?

I was delirious in my excitement. Shot-shot-shot-shot—I was like a machine gun, pelting the basket with shots. I looked down-court and saw the donor standing there watching. He was laughing. I talked with him later, and he said I was like a freight train barreling down the tracks, unstoppable. "Unbelievable," he said, laughing. "I thought you were going to bankrupt me." I used those final six hours to good avail. Even the kids who were retrieving the balls for me were spellbound. A preacher who had been standing nearby, watching all this happen, later told me, "You were insane. You were an absolute crazy man. I wish I had a video of that performance. Nobody would believe it."

It was the first time I had ever personally experienced a physical miracle in my life. I've read about them, prayed for them for others, and preached about God's healing power, and yet I was stunned by the physical transformation. No longer feeling run-down or concerned about my long-term health, I stayed on the line, winging up shot after shot, miraculously pain free.

There were a couple of miracles that day: not only my physical healing but also the increased pledge by our donor. When it was all over, I met with him. He jokingly (I hope) said he felt like he'd been duped by a con artist. Then he wrote out a check for $1.3 million. I handed it back to him and said he didn't have to do it; nobody could have known it would have amounted to so much. But he said he wanted to carry out his pledge. Overall, that crazy event raised about $2 million for the Dream Center.

If you are working in the power and authority of God— pursuing His cause for His purposes within His timetable— you have to trust that He will get you through the adventure.

More importantly, God taught me some lasting lessons that day. Maybe the most important was how necessary it is to push through those moments of doubt and pain. During those times of difficulty, God has miracles in store for you, whether physical or circumstantial.

It was an extraordinary experience emerging out of an ordinary event. That's why you cannot give up, ever. If you are working in the power and authority of God—pursuing His cause for His purposes within His timetable—you have to trust that He will get you through the adventure somehow.

Whether you're facing a seemingly impossible task or you're just overwhelmed by the magnitude or constancy of the cause itself, there are some core principles that might help you push through the hard times.

One that has enabled me to persevere over and over is the notion of giving the cause one more day. Occasionally my team has seen me return to the office feeling beaten up by the realities of the cause after a long, bruising day, only to hear me say, "I'm going to give it one more day." At that moment, that's about all I feel I have left in me: one more day's worth of energy, confidence, ability, and interest.

The trials of the cause sometimes beat the daylights out of me. But I come back the next day and realize I can handle it.

An example of a "one more day" episode was a few years ago when I was scheduled to speak at Oral Roberts University in Tulsa. We had purchased the hospital a short time before the trip, and I was already feeling the pressure of the coming payments and all the work that needed to happen in order to convert the dilapidated fifteen-story wreck into a viable ministry stronghold. On the flight from Los Angeles to Tulsa I gave God my resignation. I told Him I was finished. I realized I was incapable of pulling it off, and when I returned home, I would hand in my formal resignation from the church and retire from ministry. I remember dreading that I was probably going to go down in history as the youngest pastor in the history of the ministry to retire, since I was just twenty-three at the time.

My consolation was that by preaching at Oral Roberts University, I'd go out with a bang. Before arriving in Oklahoma, I'd already given up; in my mind, my resignation was a done deal. When I arrived in Tulsa, I checked into my room at the Hilton across the street from the ORU center where I was scheduled to preach. Nostalgically I realized this would be my swan song, my final sermon. Mentally, I had already checked out. My career as a pastor/preacher/Christian leader was as good as finished. I just had the one remaining obligation to tend to. To defray my guilt, I kept trying to convince myself that I was not a quitter but that the cause was too big for me. It was actually an act of wisdom to bow out before I really messed things up for God.

At the Hilton I handed over my luggage to the bellman, and we went toward my room. He was a middle-aged African American man, one of the nicest men I'd ever met in my life. He asked how I was doing. I lied and said I was okay. As a reflex reaction I asked how he was doing. He had a big smile and said, "Oh, I am blessed. Everything is great." As we climbed toward my floor in the elevator, he asked why I was in Tulsa. As nice as this guy was, I was in no mood to talk about my final act of ministry, so I vaguely mentioned that I would be speaking across the street. He looked at me with new interest and perked up. "Oh, you're Matthew Barnett, aren't you?" The recognition startled me. "How did you know that?" I thought maybe he had heard from the Lord. He said, "Your name's on the sign across the street." I laughed. Some days you just don't have a clue about anything.

He kept the conversation going. After a couple of moments, he asked, "Say, do you mind if I tell you my testimony?" Not what I wanted in the midst of my pity party. But unwilling to disrespect him, I told him to go ahead and let 'er rip. To my surprise, he grinned and pulled the emergency switch to stop the elevator between floors. Then he launched into his story.

"I was homeless, living on the streets, and I was away from God," he began. "I was down, I was using drugs. I was pretty much just waiting to die because I was a heroin addict. One day a group of people came by from a place called the Tulsa Dream Center. Reverend, have you ever heard of a place called the Dream Center?"

I didn't want to tell him that God had used me to start all the Dream Centers that were springing up around the country and that I was the pastor of the flagship center back in Los Angeles. I simply grunted and asked him to tell me about them.

"They came by and rescued me. They got to me and helped me put my life back together again. They restored my life and then they poured into my life. Now I've got this job and I'm blessed and my life is moving forward." He stood there with a huge smile on his face. I stood there with a bad attitude and a guilty stare. Just when I had convinced myself that nobody appreciated my dream and that everything rose and fell upon my little shoulders, this mystery man entered my life about fifteen hundred miles from home and testified about how the Dream Center had saved his life and now things were rosy.

Once he got the elevator moving again, we reached my floor and wheeled the luggage cart to my room. He led me inside, and after removing my bags from his cart, he pointed out the room's features. And then the weirdness reached another level. He watched me for a couple of seconds and then said, "Reverend, I notice you look a little tired. You mind if I pray for you?" I was still reeling from his testimony in the elevator, but how could I possibly say "no thanks" to somebody who just told me a beautiful, gut-checking story like that? I agreed and went over to one of the chairs in the room and sat down.

He said, "Let me pray for you now." Before I knew it, he pulled out from his pocket the biggest jar of anointing oil I had ever seen in my life. He opened up the jar and started walking around me, praying out loud and swiping my head with oil every time around the chair. He was praying things like, "You're a Holy Ghost man of God right now. That's right, you're a man of God! God has got great things for your life." And the whole time he was praying over me, he was circling my chair and swiping my forehead with oil. But as he continued, I felt as if he was pumping life into me. At one point he stopped directly in front of me, looked me in the eye, and asked, "Do you want the double anointing, Reverend?" I couldn't even form words to respond; I was moved to tears and simply nodded in the affirmative. He continued for a while longer and then asked if I wanted the triple anointing. Even though I'd never heard of it and was pretty sure it's not listed in the Bible, I told him it sounded good to me.

He wound up our time by anointing me with more oil and asking if I wanted the whole thing. By that time I was feeling vibrant again, so I told him, of course, I wanted all that God had for me. It was like a pep rally, and we were both getting really excited. So the two of us were in that room at the Hilton, celebrating and praising God. Finally we finished up. He left the room while I went to the bathroom to wipe off the excess oil. A few minutes later I heard a knock on the door. I opened it, and the bellman was there. "Hi, Reverend, I got so busy praying I forgot to get my tip."

Again, the experience was teaching me important lessons. There is life after giving up! You may run low on inspiration, but the dream doesn't die. The calling remains firm. You are not done giving people hope and new life until God says you're done.

Over the years I've realized that sometimes we're harder on ourselves than God is. Learn to give yourself some grace; cut yourself some slack. You have plenty of reasons to just keep showing up. After all, God called you to the task; you're not released until He releases you. A bad day, a bad week, or even a bad month is the price we pay for the privilege of doing things that change the world. Of course it's not easy. The Bible is filled with examples of great men and women who suffered for serving God, experiencing the refining fire of hardship, and then achieved eternal recognition because of their perseverance. The apostle Paul reminds us—and who would know better than him about working through trials and tribulations?—that difficulties faced along the way simply help us develop endurance, which strengthens our character and builds hope within us.[15] If you can learn lessons from those moments of disappointment or discouragement, you will be more effective because of them.

One of the most important insights about perseverance is that the pressure to quit often happens just before a major breakthrough occurs. That breakthrough might be a major step forward for the cause. It might be a radical change in the life of someone who had no hope left. In my own experience, the strongest urges to quit have always occurred just prior to something extraordinary and unexpected happening.

Earlier I described our purchase of the Queen of Angels Hospital building for $3.9 million. It was a bargain price, a real steal—except that we didn't have even 10 percent of that amount saved up. But right off the bat, God showed up and led several major donors to give us huge financial gifts that allowed us to pay for the building, free and clear.

But as I was quickly about to discover, being a property owner is not as easy as it looks. Remember, I was in my early twenties and had never owned anything other than a cheap used car. I soon found out that the monthly maintenance costs for the campus would exceed our expectations by a long shot. We ministered to the poor; even if they triple tithed, I'd be in a debtor's jail in no time. Our church did not have a building fund of accumulated cash, either; when we raised money, we spent it because the funds had been provided to help suffering people, and we were confronted with an endless stream of such individuals. But because we trusted God for the money and wholeheartedly believed that this was His provision for us to influence more lives, we worked toward the renovation of the hospital building as well as the other eight buildings on the nine-acre campus.

Let me tell you, nobody has ever had a more profound sense of buyer's remorse than I did in the weeks immediately following the closing of the sale. When my dad and I had first toured the hospital—and every time we walked its corridors up through the closing of the deal—all I could see was life-changing potential. Once we owned the building, all I could see was a terrifying, 400,000-square-foot mess that represented the biggest mistake made in the history of mankind. Instead of life-changing potential I saw a mountain of debt, an insurmountable monthly sum to raise, years of reconstruction required to make the building habitable, and countless hours of haggling with the city government over building regulations. I was certain that I had signed a contract for the biggest noose that had ever been put around a man's neck. And each night I felt that rope getting a little bit tighter.

While lying in bed one night, unable to sleep because of the monstrosity I had just purchased, the pressure was so intense that I felt as if the devil were lying in that bed next to me. He was whispering things like, "You're a total failure," and, "This monument to yourself is going to tear you apart," right into my ear. "You will be the laughingstock of the ministry world, Matthew Barnett. They'll remember you for a long time to come." It felt as if a five-hundred-pound brick was pressing down on my body, and the heaviness of the situation was squeezing the life out of me.

Later that week I entered the building again and surveyed the hanging wallpaper, the ripped-up floors, the holes in the walls, and the hanging light fixtures, and I felt the breeze from the wind that was whistling through the broken windows. I walked to the nearest corner of the room, slumped down on the floor with my back against the wall, put my head in my hands, and rocked back and forth with my eyes closed. "What did I do? What was I thinking?" Those thoughts kept racing through my brain. I let loose all the pent-up emotions and totally lost it. I owned the building, but doubt and fear owned me.

God met me in that corner. He gave me the impression that everything would be fine if I'd trust Him and simply take the first little step toward using the resources and doing what had to be done to make this a place that could heal broken lives. My dad and I had prayed for hour after hour seeking God's guidance prior to closing the deal, and we truly felt He was in it with us. We had seen the building as a means of touching people's lives with love and hope. Nothing had changed except for my heart. The heart can deceive us and often does. And it was doing so at that moment. God was setting me straight. All I had to do was trust Him, hold on to the big dream, and take the first small steps forward.

Recalling God's words to me a few nights earlier, I took a deep breath and walked the perimeter of the campus. I'd stop every few yards and pan the property from a new angle. Each time I forced myself to say, "Look at this complex. Imagine all the things God can do here. Think about how many people can have their shattered lives put back together by His love right here, in the center of Los Angeles. What good has come from LA in recent years? From now on, greatness will come from this place." As my confidence grew, I sensed a renewed passion that had been destroyed by the fear. And I remembered the miracles God had pulled off to help us purchase the building in the first place. Surely this was not some supernatural joke. God was in the business of healing lives, and He had called me to do this with Him. He was serious. I needed to be too.

As our initial act of trust, we made the first floor livable and moved thirty-five people in soon thereafter. It wasn't easy. The first time we turned on the water, the pipes burst and flooded the floor. I had another crying spell. Not too long afterward, we got an estimate for what it would cost to install city-mandated sprinklers throughout the building. I nearly had a heart attack.

In the meantime we were renovating the other eight buildings that were part of the campus. They were not exactly poised for a cover story in *Architectural Digest* when we took control of them, either. Somewhere along the way I considered changing the name from the Dream Center to the Money Pit.

To keep funds flowing for both the most important aspect of our lives (serving people) and the tool we believed would eventually expand our capacity to do so (the renovation of the buildings), I began taking every outside speaking gig I could get. We contacted conferences and churches everywhere, asking if they'd let me come and speak about the great work God was doing at the Dream Center. I was very honest about the situation, too, because I was essentially begging them to help me deal with that financial boulder I was carting around all day. I offered to pay my way to their church and preach for free if they'd let me take and keep an offering after I was done. We were desperate. I believed God was going to do a great work through all this, but I knew I could not simply sit around and wait for Him to do another miracle. If we were partners in this cause, I had to do my share. So I did.

Suddenly, as word got out, we had a lot of churches sending people to volunteer with us, and many of those churches gave us money. We started to get checks out of the blue, from pastors and churches we'd never interacted with, who were trying to encourage us. We latched on to the idea of describing the Dream Center as "the church America is building," hoping to inspire people nationwide to feel some ownership in what we were doing in Los Angeles and perhaps to build on our model in their own city. Churches began sending us mission support funds. Youth groups came for extended stays, went home, spread the word, and more funds came in. I was calling everybody I'd ever known—friends, relatives, classmates—and asking them if they could spare fifty bucks, or a hundred, or even just ten, to help us along. Eventually there was enough of a groundswell of little sources of revenue trickling in that we were able to make a dent in the renovation work.

You may want to give up at any of a hundred points along the way. The Lord knows I sure wanted to! But you have to hold tightly to the dream and realize that expanding your influence is like climbing a mountain: the closer to the top you get, the harder it is to make progress. Occasionally you'll hit a plateau, and you'll stay there for a while. That's okay; it allows you to acclimate and regroup for the next push forward. You won't always move ahead at the same speed, and there will be days when the best you can do is maintain the ground you previously captured. The more you can fall in love with the effort you're making rather than obsessing about the results you achieve, the more enjoyable and productive the journey will be.

My good buddy and colleague-in-the-cause Aaron Jayne talks about how he has learned to persevere by having joy. He recalls some words of wisdom that my father gave us when we were starting out, a couple of know-nothing twentysomething goobers in the big city. He warned us that if you don't learn to have fun and enjoy the ride, you'll burn out. You can only work eighty hours a week for so long before you lose your passion and squander your potential.

So besides working crazy hours and taking on things we knew nothing about, we have sought to have a life beyond our cause. That does not diminish our passion for the cause; in many ways, it has kept us fresh and alive so we can stay focused on it. Certainly we get a real kick out of serving people, but it can be mentally, emotionally, physically, and spiritually draining, no matter how much we love it or how good we might be at it.

Everyone has different ways of releasing steam; you have to have something that enables you to recover from the pressures of pursuing your cause. Some people will refer to this as having balance in life; we tend to think of it as simply having a life. A lot of us have incorporated sports as an outlet. At the Dream Center we offer a lot of organized sports activities and contests, including softball, volleyball, beach volleyball, basketball, and other intramural sports. We try to take advantage of the entertainment activities available throughout the city, and we have a lot of musical events on our campus. We take trips to Dodgers and Lakers games. You get the idea. You need healthy diversions to clear your head and keep your body tuned for the stresses and challenges of the cause.

Here's one final thought about how to persevere: never lose sight of the victories and the landmark experiences that God grants you.

Victories? I love to walk the campus, stop somebody I haven't seen for a while, and ask what God is doing in his or her life. I absolutely glow when I encounter a teenage girl who joined us as a strung-out drug addict who once again has a sparkle in her eyes as she excitedly shows me her arm, healed from where needle marks used to be. I love hearing the testimony of a twenty-year-old young man who was turned out on the streets before even reaching high school. Once caught up in the gang life, he now dreams of saving his peers from a life of crime and ugliness. I think of the beautiful young woman who was on the road to self-destruction during her teen years and kept it hidden from her parents, only to lose her will to live once she became addicted to OxyContin. But now in the final stages of our recovery program, she is on the right track and rushes over to tell me about her dream of going to Africa as a missionary. I look forward to seeing the people from my adopted block and finding out how their lives are going. I look out at the sea of faces I've come to know and love at Angelus Temple and think about all the people who have given their lives to Christ there and are giving themselves to others in service. I watch Alena Strickland as she loves the mentally and physically disabled children in her care. I know that come this Wednesday and Saturday, Emilio and Karina Cervantes will be sharing the love of Christ in the housing project where they were more likely to be killed than welcomed before they began their amazing work there.

Never lose sight of the victories and the landmark experiences that God grants you.

If I try even just a little bit, I can easily fill an afternoon reliving memory after memory of people whose lives have been touched and changed by the Dream Center. I am not responsible for the turn-around and the impact of their lives, but the Lord has given me the privilege of partnering with Him in touching those lives.

Landmarks? I think back to the dark days following my crash-and-burn experience preaching at the age of sixteen—and how that propelled me to a new level of ministry. I think about the hardship of landing in Los Angeles and the Echo Park experience that broke me, then healed me. I recall the long nights of worry over the new campus and how God came in and set me straight. I replay in my mind that night spent on skid row, where I learned new things about street life and felt my passion increase to new heights. I think about what God has done in the life of a passionate but underwhelming kid from the desert who came to the big city and has tried to listen to and obey God. The transformation in my own life has been breathtaking.

When I reflect on these kinds of victories and landmarks, the point is not that I have done something great. I haven't. The point is that God invited and allowed me to partner with Him and many others on a journey of unimaginable proportions. He has delivered striking results that make my occasional fears, doubts, sacrifices, and hardships worthwhile. When I touch these memories, I cannot fantasize anything better. These memories—and the prospect of being able to create new ones like them for a long time to come—are sufficient to fuel me through the tough times.

What are the landmarks and victories that can lift you out of the doldrums and despair of everyday struggles? In your modesty, do not fail to catalogue these milestones in your mind and heart. The purpose of remembering them is not to inflate your ego; it is to remind you that the cause within you still lives. Giving up on that cause is simply not an option.

WHAT I'VE LEARNED

- You will encounter the urge to quit many times. Get over it. Quitting is not an option; always be prepared to give it one more day.
- The urge to quit is strongest just before breakthroughs occur. Those are the times when it's most important to stay focused and committed.
- Pursuing a cause is difficult. Cut yourself some slack along the way; God does.
- If you truly believe you are working in partnership with God, trust Him.

- Avoid burnout; work hard at pursuing and fulfilling your cause, but have a life, too.
- When you have discouraging times, review the landmarks and victories that make the cause worth pursuing.

CHAPTER 11

THE PLEASURES OF PURSUING YOUR CAUSE

LIVING LIFE WITHOUT GOD'S DREAM at the center isn't much of a life. One person who knows that even better than I do is Jim Bakker, the televangelist who spent five years in prison and saw his entire life, family, and ministry crumble in a high-profile descent from fame and influence to heartbreak and hopelessness.

I mention Jim because he is part of the Dream Center's extended family. Many people are not aware that soon after he was released from prison, he was invited out to my dad's church to see his son, Jamie, graduate from one of their programs. Jim was reluctant to make the trip from North Carolina, where he was living a simple but lonely life in a secluded farmhouse, to Phoenix, where he would be sitting in the midst of a pastor's conference.

"I didn't want to embarrass Tommy," Jim said. "He had come to visit me in prison and had been encouraging me all along the way. The last thing I wanted to do was cause him any pain or embarrassment.

Tommy is a dreamer. And he elevated and encouraged me. I had stopped dreaming. The little boy inside me was gone, and there were no more dreams. I had nothing to work toward."

My father convinced Jim to make the trip to see his son graduate from the program. Jamie gave a stirring speech that left Jim in a puddle of tears in the back of the auditorium. While Jim was visiting Phoenix, my dad talked to him about a big abandoned hospital in Los Angeles that he and I were exploring for our ministry in LA. My father mentioned that one of these days Jim should join him out there to check it out. Jim filed it away in the back of his mind and then returned to his isolated life in North Carolina.

Sometime later a local ministry invited Jim to Los Angeles to speak to a group that helps young women whose lives are in disarray. Somehow my dad found out about that trip and invited Jim to come by and see the Dream Center. By that time we had purchased the hospital and were expanding our work. Jim arrived in time to witness our weekly Thursday night service in the gymnasium. Without warning, my dad called Jim up on the stage and asked him to speak to the group. Jim was still a very hopeless man who had been devastated by the demeaning years in prison and his widespread rejection by the church.

"When I got out of prison, I was a broken man. The guards and others call you names and put you down and make you feel worthless," Jim explained. "The nasty words kept boomeranging in my head. Prison does nothing for your self-worth. They just teach you that you're nothing, that you have no future. When I was released, I never had any plans to ever, ever preach again. I didn't know what I was going to do, but I knew it wouldn't be preaching."

When God shows up, you just cannot top what He produces.

If Jim's time in prison was as low as the valleys get, I'd bet that his time at our midweek service was close to the top of the mountain.

He very reluctantly agreed to speak to our people. It turned into one of those magical evenings that nobody expects and nobody can plan. When God shows up, you just cannot top what He produces. Jim remembers:

In prison I couldn't speak. They had a Toastmasters Club there, and I went to the meetings, but I couldn't speak. All my life I'd been communicating, but by the time I got to prison, I couldn't even put words together. The trauma of going to prison was just too much. But that night when I was visiting the Dream Center, Tommy called me up to preach, and as I did, an anointing came upon me that was incredible. I had thought I'd never preach again, but that night was really something. The crowd was giving me standing ovations and shouting "Amen."

I was telling them about life in prison and about how God got me out of prison. I was supposed to die in prison—I had a forty-five-year sentence—but I was out after five years. I looked out at the crowd at the Dream Center, and I said, "Have any of you ever been in prison?" And three-quarters of the crowd stood up! I said, "Oh my, I'm home. These are my people!" You know, when you're an inmate, it becomes like a fraternity, you just bond. You have a language that you get. Words like *dawg*. I didn't know *dawg*. My first day of prison one of the inmates handed me something to autograph, and he said, "Sign this, 'To My Road Dawg,'" and I had no idea what he was saying. I asked him, "Is that dirty?" But at the Dream Center I met a lot of my dawgs, which I learned means "good friend." That night was just remarkable.

The love Jim felt from the assembled people that night was a critical step in receiving the healing God wanted for him. He stayed overnight with us, and my dad gave him a tour of our ministry the next morning. He met all kinds of people, with all types of checkered backgrounds, and felt comfortable. He had been picked up the previous day and brought to our campus by Armondo. This ex-gang member had first joined one at age seven and is the only known individual to leave the 18th Street Gang without dying from natural causes or gang-inflicted violence. When Armondo saw Jim on campus the next day, he came up to Jim, gave him a big hug, and told him how much he loved Jim. It brought tears to Jim's eyes. In fact, many of the Dream Center people he ran into during the course of the tour told Jim they loved and appreciated him. He said he had never felt so wanted and loved—a feeling that, like preaching, he had believed he would never experience again in his life.

At the end of the tour, Jim quietly asked my dad if he could stay one more day. Of course his request was granted, so he went off and served people with the Hope for the Homeless team. The next day he asked to stay overnight again, which he did, enabling him to serve with a couple of other teams the next day. He returned to ask if he could stay one more night, did so, and then served with still more teams the next day.

One thing led to another, and Jim wound up staying with us for many months. He led Bible study groups, spoke to various groups of people in recovery, engaged in street ministry, and was active in Adopt-A-Block. Much more happened through his time at the Dream Center—it was an amazing time that he and his wife have written about—but my point is that the simple act of serving people facilitates God's cause within you. If you have never known your cause, serving flushes it out. If you had been pursuing your cause but life crushed it, serving has the power to rekindle that flame of passion. You may think it doesn't exist or that it's gone, but the more you imitate Jesus and love people by addressing their needs, the more likely you are to find that cause bubbling to the surface. That's exactly what happened to Jim Bakker, and he is still passionately pursuing that cause today, more than a decade after his time with us.

By the way, Jim Bakker is one of the pioneers of Christian broadcasting. In the 1960s, he started the talk show *The 700 Club*, which Pat Robertson later took over. He was a founder of the Trinity Broadcasting Network (TBN). He was instrumental in launching other significant media ministries in addition to his well-known PTL broadcast and cable television network. All of those efforts reflect the dream that God originally placed in Jim's heart of using media to reach the world for Christ. His years of hardship squelched the dream. After he was loved back into service, the cause reappeared in his mind and heart. He is now pursuing it wholeheartedly through Morningside Media Masters Commission, located in the Ozarks in Missouri, training young people to use the power of the media to reach young generations for Christ.

Like Jim, thousands of other people have experienced the restorative power of a cause. My dad once made a comment I'll never forget. After the Dream Center was up and running, he thanked me for pursuing that type of ministry. I was perplexed by his words and asked what he meant. "Being connected with this cause has added years to my life. Here I am, in my sixties, and I feel alive again. Starting this work has breathed new life into me." Since then I've noticed how many people in the latter stages of their lives—people in their sixties, seventies, and eighties—come alive when they are involved in outreach activities. Serving people gives you a greater motivation to keep on living.

The cause that God places inside your heart never dies. You may go through rough patches in your life, but that cause will remain part of your spiritual DNA. It will always be there to guide you to a place of meaning, direction, impact, and joy. Pursuing the cause can breathe life back into your heart and soul. It is another one of God's special gifts to you.

One way to know if you are truly living for your cause is to figure out whether your life is producing happiness or joy. There's a big difference. One of the rewards of living for your cause is that it frees you from being bound only to what makes you happy. You see, happiness is about taking care of yourself. What makes you happy? For most Americans it includes living in comfort, belonging to the right groups, attending special events, having lots of resources at your disposal, and building a good reputation. Those things create their own type of bondage that delivers a temporary form of happiness. It's temporary because you have to keep working at it to reproduce it and maintain your standing.

But God's desire is for you to get your eyes off yourself and onto others—not the stuff they have that you want, but the needs they have that you can address. That's what God did for you through Jesus. When you invest yourself fully in your cause, the end result is joy—a lasting sense of peace and comfort that redefines your life.

Joy comes from knowing that people are better off because of the value you have added to their lives.

Joy comes from knowing that people are better off because of the value you have added to their lives. You may have prayed for them, or you may have given them a million dollars; what matters is not how the world measures the magnitude of your gift but that you have sacrificed something of your life for theirs.

Katie Holloway knows about the joy received from serving through her cause. She is young—in her early twenties—but has already established a track record of doing whatever it takes to serve the kind of people God has placed on her radar—in her case, it is underprivileged children. When she came to Los Angeles, she wasn't yet aware of that calling, but over the past few years it has become clear, and she has wasted no time in that pursuit:

> When I came to Los Angeles from my home in Florida, my intention was just to finish college at Cal State and then get a job. After months of looking for a church home, my mom suggested I try the Dream Center. I fell in love with the church the first time I attended. After being at the Dream Center for about a year, I began to get such a heart and a burden for homeless children while serving in Adopt-A-Block and some of the different youth ministries.
>
> I started visiting the homeless shelters and saw the brokenness among the children there. They would just run up to me and hug me and not let go. They didn't know me from Adam, but they craved attention and someone to tell them it was going to be okay. They wanted people to look at them and not think they were just these oddballs in society. After seeing these children and hearing their stories, my heart was totally broken. I became consumed with the thoughts and images of the children I had seen. The passion built up within me to see these youth and kids change.
>
> My parents had started a camp for homeless children back home, and I felt the Lord calling me to start one in California. Despite my longing to start a camp, at first I figured it was something I couldn't really do because of my age. But after watching all these young people serve, seeing Pastor Matthew's heart, and hearing how he came to Los Angeles when he was twenty and had this huge vision to do something nobody ever thought could happen—it really inspired me. I knew I had to step out in that same kind of faith.

My first year, as I was starting out, I was almost nineteen. I shared the vision with a friend of mine, and she was extremely supportive. But I didn't know many people in Orange County or LA, and I was petrified because I thought, *Who am I to start calling shelters and churches and convincing them that this is something we're going to do?* I felt sure people were going to laugh in my face when I said I was going to do something about the people in shelters who were in their own backyards.

So many times people would say, "You're too young. You're just a college student." Or, "You do not know anyone." Or, "The financial stability you will need is something you can't manage. You're barely making it yourself." Even my parents, who are very supportive, sometimes asked things like, "Katie, is this something you really want to do? Do you really believe you can do this?" But I knew in my heart it was something God was calling me to do. And I believe that when you take those first steps of faith, the Lord really does put people in your life who get it and will help guide and direct you.

I remember in the beginning calling about five shelters, explaining the camp, and asking them, "Is this something you would want to do?" I couldn't believe I was saying that to them because the start of the camp was just three months away and I had no money, no volunteers, no churches behind this, and yet I was telling these shelters we were going to do it. I remember hanging up the phone and thinking, *What did I just say?* I had never done anything like that. I always have a plan, no matter what I'm doing. But the people from these shelters were just thanking me over and over. Some directors were crying on the phone with me, saying, "People don't understand

the needs, the importance. No one helps." They were so
excited.

I took a step of faith and contacted a church in Orange
County that owned a campground. The church not only
allowed us to use their facilities, they did not even charge
us for doing so. Then I began contacting other churches
and college groups, and soon many people were offering
to volunteer or provide financial support. After that first
step of faith, I would meet someone at a Bible study or at a
coffee shop, and it was like divine appointment after divine
appointment, where God was opening the doors for us. I
still got a lot of rejections and people telling me it wasn't
possible, but sometimes that just fueled my fire.

So we began Camp Joy in 2006, when I was just about
nineteen. We take the children from Los Angeles and Orange
County who are living in emergency shelters or are in hiding
or transitional housing from abusive fathers or mothers. We
take them to a three-night/four-day camp, where each child
gets a one-on-one mentor. During those four days, the kids
are loved and served and poured into. Each night we have a
big event or a youth service.

These kids have nothing in life. They usually sleep on cots
or gymnastic mats in these huge rooms in the shelters. So
we give them sleeping bags, bags of cool clothes, backpacks
and school supplies, and really anything we can think of
that will bless them. And when they go back to the shelters,
we match these kids with a mentor for a year so that they're
not just coming to camp and then having to go home and
live life by themselves. We want them to find their cause.
We want them to know they can overcome generational
homelessness, and we try to help them with that. We try to
help them find a solution to overcome their circumstances

and discover their own cause. Society is telling them they're going to end up in the same mess as their parents. We want them to see they can break the cycle.

So I did this during my college years, in addition to finishing college and working full-time. There were definitely times that I felt I couldn't go on or I couldn't do this, but you know, God always supplied and opened the next door. I just graduated from college this past May, and we're still doing the camp and going strong. In summer 2010, we expanded to two camps, holding a three-day/four-night session called The Avenue for teenagers. Again, people told us we were absolutely out of our minds, since that meant raising about $60,000. I know by Dream Center standards that is a small amount, but I looked at that number sometimes and felt as if I'd have a heart attack. By the end of 2010, though, we had served hundreds of kids and teens from ten homeless shelters in Los Angeles and Orange County.

It's been a great learning process. I have always been a type A person, but the Lord kind of stopped me in my tracks to do this camp, and it's been a day-by-day journey of trusting Him. Even when I graduated, normally I would have felt I had to have my future all lined up, but it isn't. That petrified me, but learning to lean on the Lord has been the number-one lesson for me, that and constantly going back to seek His counsel and being open and willing to follow. God is always speaking and trying to teach us about the causes in our lives; if we're listening and obedient, stepping out in faith, we'll do things we never thought we were capable of doing.

I look back to four years ago, and I'm so glad I listened and took the steps of faith that seemed ridiculous. The whole experience has taught me so much and brought me to a place I've been so thankful for. I really thought I was going to do this camp just one summer, but it has affected my life in every aspect. It even affected my future. I wanted to work in the corporate world, but about halfway through my degree I changed. I feel called to ministry and to the nonprofit world, figuring out what can be done to affect communities. This has changed my life.

And Katie has changed a lot of other people's lives too. As she admits, her hope of changing people has changed her, and she has experienced joy beyond her expectations.

That joy of fulfilling your cause is something I am privileged to experience more often than you'd probably believe. I remember the day I wanted to do something to bless the kids of the homeless families living at the Dream Center. I called the director of our program to these families and asked her to round up all the kids and meet me at Build-A-Bear in Hollywood. I was expecting maybe fifteen or twenty children to be there, a good-size gathering. I got there a few minutes after they arrived and wondered where all these children were coming from. There were about fifty kids from our homeless families. Fifty! I didn't realize we had that many. I was thinking, *Oh my goodness! Let's see, fifty children at $40 each, that's* . . . But it didn't really matter to me. The wonderful thing was how many kids would be blessed by this off-the-cuff adventure.

You see, the mathematic calculations in my head ceased the minute I started watching these kids. They saw me, and suddenly it was pandemonium. They started hugging me and shouting, "We get to go to Build-A-Bear today! We get to go to Build-A-Bear today!" For a lot of them it was their first time. My kids have been there so often, it's not even that big a deal for them anymore. But for these children, it was a lifetime memory in the making.

The woman from the store took over and started getting the kids to select and make their bears. Watching their faces and hearing their enthusiasm was priceless. They choose the bear, the other parts of their animals, and then they followed the lady's instructions on how to put it all together. She had them rub the heart of the bear to get it going, and the kids were rubbing away. Then they did a little dance and jump. It was too good for words; I didn't want the process to end. Then came the time to clean their bears and name them. I was circulating among the kids, talking to them about their bears and the names they wanted and generally having the time of my life.

I got to one tiny African American girl, probably about six years old, and noticed she had a male bear. "Hey, you've got a boy bear. You didn't want to make a special princess bear? What kind of bear are you making?" She looked up at me and said, "I'm making a Pastor Matthew Superhero Bear." I started tearing up, right in front of her, and told her how phenomenal that was, and hugged her and thanked her. She gave me that bear and said, "I made this for you, Pastor. The Pastor Matthew Superhero Bear."

Where did that come from in that little girl's heart? Oh man, she wiped me out! Once again I realized that I need those people more than they need me and that they have brought me a level of joy and fulfillment I would never experience anywhere else. And what did it take? Listening to the Holy Spirit, being obedient, and simply loving them. How tough is that? And how can you get a better return on your investment? I mean, come on: a handmade Pastor Matthew Superhero Bear? It doesn't get better than that.

You can experience joy through your cause when you are finally done with yourself and focused on others. The world will describe your efforts as sacrificial and your motives as selfless. You probably won't see it that way. To you it will simply be doing whatever it takes to pursue the cause that defines who you are and that compels you to keep going each day. The good feelings you get are not from the public attention you attract or the awards you receive. They are from being consistent with who God made you to be and from reaping the joy of seeing God honored and people loved.

You will never finish your cause. You will not outlive your cause. If it ever seems to be coming to a close, you can bet that the cause will morph into a new way of serving people that builds on what you've already experienced. Your cause was made to consume you. When it does, you become like the sun, a blazing ball of energy that illuminates and brings life to a world of frozen hearts and souls.

One paraphrase of Proverbs 29:18 reads, "If people can't see what God is doing, they stumble all over themselves; but when they attend to what he reveals, they are most blessed" (THE MESSAGE). Another translation notes that without a revelation from God, people go wild, ignoring all limitations or boundaries. They make their own rules and develop their own paths.

Look around. You'll see that our society is littered with people who have no sense of Christ in our culture or their own redemptive role within this world. There are millions of people who have not bothered to identify the reason God placed them here. They have chosen not to invest any time or energy in determining what special purpose and outcomes He has ordained for them. If you doubt this, simply examine the prisons, the streets, the boardrooms, and the classrooms. You'll witness a constant reality: numerous people meander through their lives in a desperate but ill-defined search for meaning and impact. Thankfully, others have found lasting meaning and impact through the God-given cause that He placed within them.

> Your cause was made to consume you. When it does, you become like the sun, a blazing ball of energy that illuminates and brings life to a world of frozen hearts and souls.

Can you see what God is doing—or, perhaps, what He wants to do—in your life? Is your life sufficiently disciplined by an awareness of the grand purpose for which you were created? Are you increasingly committed to fulfilling that dream?

Think of your cause as a holy gift from God. It is, after all, *the cause of Christ.* When you are absorbed by that cause, you are in the sweet spot of your life, intent upon honoring Christ by loving others into greater well-being. When I was young, old-time preachers used to exhort us to give our lives to the cause of Christ. Even before I fully understood what that meant, I knew it was big and special. It was something I wanted. I could not define it concretely, but I knew it had to do with living a transformed, exciting life. It was a life bigger than simply receiving a "Get Out of Hell Free" card.

Now, having been in hot pursuit of that cause for nearly three decades, I can assure you that the cause of Christ offers a life of adventure and excitement. It is a life conducted on the edge, an existence that is heroic in the right sense. The cause of Christ is grandiose, and its magnificence is left wanting without your wholehearted engagement. Your share of the cause of Christ catapults you beyond success to eternal significance. It is a cause that is far beyond your mortal ability, yet woefully incomplete without your contribution. The cause of Christ is an incomparable one, and you are a vital part of it.

There are two paths, but just one choice.

Which path will you choose?

Related Scripture Passages

THE BIBLE IS FULL OF PASSAGES that address the importance and process of finding the cause within you. Listed below are some of the passages that have been helpful to me. Each passage stands on its own, yet reading all of these, from the first to the last, can be an informative and motivating journey in itself! Take a few minutes to read the passages, reflecting on their relevance to your life and thinking about what God is saying to you.

I SAMUEL 10:20-23

When Samuel brought all the tribes of Israel near, the tribe of Benjamin was chosen. Then he brought forward the tribe of Benjamin, clan by clan, and Matri's clan was chosen. Finally Saul son of Kish was chosen. But when they looked for him, he was not to be found. So they inquired further of the LORD, "Has the man come here yet?" And the LORD said, "Yes, he has hidden himself among the baggage." They ran and brought him out, and as he stood among the people he was a head taller than any of the others. (NIV)

PROVERBS 1:7

Fear of the LORD is the foundation of true knowledge, but fools despise wisdom and discipline.

PROVERBS 3:5-7

Trust in the LORD with all your heart; do not depend on your own understanding. Seek his will in all you do, and he will show you which path to take. Don't be impressed with your own wisdom. Instead, fear the LORD and turn away from evil.

PROVERBS 29:18

Where there is no revelation, the people cast off restraint; but blessed is he who keeps the law. (NIV)

ISAIAH 1:17

Learn to do good. Seek justice. Help the oppressed. Defend the cause of orphans. Fight for the rights of widows.

ISAIAH 55:8-9

"For my thoughts are not your thoughts, neither are your ways my ways," declares the LORD. "As the heavens are higher than the earth, so are my ways higher than your ways and my thoughts than your thoughts." (NIV)

JEREMIAH 17:9

The heart is deceitful above all things and beyond cure. Who can understand it? (NIV)

JEREMIAH 29:11-13
"For I know the plans I have for you," says the LORD. "They are plans for good and not for disaster, to give you a future and a hope. In those days when you pray, I will listen. If you look for me wholeheartedly, you will find me."

MATTHEW 6:33-34
Seek the Kingdom of God above all else, and live righteously, and he will give you everything you need. So don't worry about tomorrow, for tomorrow will bring its own worries. Today's trouble is enough for today.

MATTHEW 7:12
So in everything, do to others what you would have them do to you, for this sums up the Law and the Prophets. (NIV)

MATTHEW 11:28-30
Come to me, all you who are weary and burdened, and I will give you rest. Take my yoke upon you and learn from me, for I am gentle and humble in heart, and you will find rest for your souls. For my yoke is easy and my burden is light. (NIV)

MATTHEW 12:30-31
He who is not with me is against me, and he who does not gather with me scatters. And so I tell you, every sin and blasphemy will be forgiven men, but the blasphemy against the Spirit will not be forgiven. (NIV)

MATTHEW 19:26
With God everything is possible.

MATTHEW 23:11-12

The greatest among you must be a servant. But those who exalt themselves will be humbled, and those who humble themselves will be exalted.

MATTHEW 25:21

The master was full of praise. "Well done, my good and faithful servant. You have been faithful in handling this small amount, so now I will give you many more responsibilities. Let's celebrate together!"

MARK 12:30-31

"And you must love the LORD your God with all your heart, all your soul, all your mind, and all your strength." The second is equally important: "Love your neighbor as yourself." No other commandment is greater than these.

LUKE 5:10-11

Then Jesus said to Simon, "Don't be afraid; from now on you will catch men." So they pulled their boats up on shore, left everything and followed him. (NIV)

LUKE 12:48

When someone has been given much, much will be required in return; and when someone has been entrusted with much, even more will be required.

LUKE 16:10

If you are faithful in little things, you will be faithful in large ones. But if you are dishonest in little things, you won't be honest with greater responsibilities.

LUKE 19:11-27

The crowd was listening to everything Jesus said. And because he was nearing Jerusalem, he told them a story to correct the impression that the Kingdom of God would begin right away. He said, "A nobleman was called away to a distant empire to be crowned king and then return. Before he left, he called together ten of his servants and divided among them ten pounds of silver, saying, 'Invest this for me while I am gone.' But his people hated him and sent a delegation after him to say, 'We do not want him to be our king.' After he was crowned king, he returned and called in the servants to whom he had given the money. He wanted to find out what their profits were. The first servant reported, 'Master, I invested your money and made ten times the original amount!' 'Well done!' the king exclaimed. 'You are a good servant. You have been faithful with the little I entrusted to you, so you will be governor of ten cities as your reward.' The next servant reported, 'Master, I invested your money and made five times the original amount.' 'Well done!' the king said. 'You will be governor over five cities.' But the third servant brought back only the original amount of money and said, 'Master, I hid your money and kept it safe. I was afraid because you are a hard man to deal with, taking what isn't yours and harvesting crops you didn't plant.' 'You wicked servant!' the king roared. 'Your own words condemn you. If you knew that I'm a hard man who takes what isn't mine and harvests crops I didn't plant, why didn't you deposit my money in the bank? At least I could have gotten some interest on it.' Then, turning to the others standing nearby, the king ordered, 'Take the money from this servant, and give it to the one who has ten pounds.' 'But, master,' they said, 'he already has ten pounds!' 'Yes,' the king replied, 'and to those who use well what they are given, even more will be given. But from those who do nothing, even what little they have will be taken away. And as for these enemies of mine who

*didn't want me to be their king—bring them in and execute them
right here in front of me.'"*

JOHN 5:1-9
*Some time later, Jesus went up to Jerusalem for a feast of the Jews.
Now there is in Jerusalem near the Sheep Gate a pool, which in
Aramaic is called Bethesda and which is surrounded by five covered
colonnades. Here a great number of disabled people used to lie—the
blind, the lame, the paralyzed. One who was there had been an
invalid for thirty-eight years. When Jesus saw him lying there and
learned that he had been in this condition for a long time, he asked
him, "Do you want to get well?" "Sir," the invalid replied, "I have
no one to help me into the pool when the water is stirred. While
I am trying to get in, someone else goes down ahead of me." Then
Jesus said to him, "Get up! Pick up your mat and walk." At once
the man was cured; he picked up his mat and walked.* (NIV)

ACTS 20:24
*But my life is worth nothing to me unless I use it for finishing the
work assigned me by the Lord Jesus.*

ROMANS 5:3-5
*Not only so, but we also rejoice in our sufferings, because we know
that suffering produces perseverance; perseverance, character; and
character, hope. And hope does not disappoint us, because God has
poured out his love into our hearts by the Holy Spirit, whom he has
given us.* (NIV)

ROMANS 8:28
*And we know that God causes everything to work together for the
good of those who love God and are called according to his purpose
for them.*

ROMANS 8:31
If God is for us, who can ever be against us?

ROMANS 12:1-2
I plead with you to give your bodies to God because of all he has done for you. Let them be a living and holy sacrifice—the kind he will find acceptable. This is truly the way to worship him. Don't copy the behavior and customs of this world, but let God transform you into a new person by changing the way you think. Then you will learn to know God's will for you, which is good and pleasing and perfect.

ROMANS 12:9
Don't just pretend to love others. Really love them.

I CORINTHIANS 12:7
A spiritual gift is given to each of us so we can help each other.

I CORINTHIANS 12:28-31
Here are some of the parts God has appointed for the church: first are apostles, second are prophets, third are teachers, then those who do miracles, those who have the gift of healing, those who can help others, those who have the gift of leadership, those who speak in unknown languages. Are we all apostles? Are we all prophets? Are we all teachers? Do we all have the power to do miracles? Do we all have the gift of healing? Do we all have the ability to speak in unknown languages? Do we all have the ability to interpret unknown languages? Of course not! So you should earnestly desire the most helpful gifts.

I CORINTHIANS 15:58
Be strong and immovable. Always work enthusiastically for the Lord, for you know that nothing you do for the Lord is ever useless.

GALATIANS 5:22-23

The Holy Spirit produces this kind of fruit in our lives: love, joy, peace, patience, kindness, goodness, faithfulness, gentleness, and self-control. There is no law against these things!

PHILIPPIANS 4:6

Don't worry about anything; instead, pray about everything. Tell God what you need, and thank him for all he has done.

COLOSSIANS 3:23

Work willingly at whatever you do, as though you were working for the Lord rather than for people.

JAMES 1:27

Religion that God our Father accepts as pure and faultless is this: to look after orphans and widows in their distress and to keep oneself from being polluted by the world. (NIV)

JAMES 3:13

If you are wise and understand God's ways, prove it by living an honorable life, doing good works with the humility that comes from wisdom.

1 JOHN 4:18

Such love has no fear, because perfect love expels all fear. If we are afraid, it is for fear of punishment, and this shows that we have not fully experienced his perfect love.

Acknowledgments

MATTHEW would like to thank the following people:

The amazing George Barna, who spent hours upon hours listening to me ramble about my cause while smiling the entire time, listening with such interest. Your desire to capture this story from the beginning, going on tours of the Dream Center, interviewing people—clearly, this wasn't just a book to you; it's a life's mission, a reflection of a core value.

My beautiful wife, Caroline, who is more enthusiastic about this cause than I am and radiates more love than anyone could ever comprehend. You rocked my world when you came to volunteer and pour your heart out to the people on the streets. I love you!

My little kids, Mia and Caden, for always sprinting through the house when I come home, yelling, "Daddy, Daddy!" I love you kids! (Make sure you're just as wonderful when you're teenagers!)

My brother, Luke, the most dynamic church builder and my best friend! One day I'll have the round of my life and beat you in golf.

My sister, Kristie, my other best friend, whose energy and enthusiasm for life can be felt from a mile away. You show us all how to have an invigorated life.

My mom, Marja Barnett, the coolest mom of all time. Remember when you used to tee-pee houses with me and my friends? You were always the sweetest, hippest mom around—and the one who never stopped praying for me.

My father, Tommy Barnett, who has walked with me through the fire every day at the Dream Center. You will always be "the Godfather of the Dream Center."

My wonderful church family, Angelus Temple, the liveliest congregation known to mankind. I thank God that you are always ready to start another ministry. And I am grateful to the Foursquare family for investing in the temple renovation.

The one-year volunteers, the one-week volunteers, the people by the thousands who have given their lives to live in an old hospital and get up every morning and pay the price of servanthood.

My assistant, Todd—well, what can I say? You are the nerd I need in my life to get things done. And you are the radical man who found the cause from within.

Esther Fedorkevich, you took a chance on me by representing this project. You are absolutely the best!

The Tyndale family: wow, you not only believe in this project, but your staff even came halfway across the country to serve here with us! What a class organization.

Michael and Dru Hammer, thanks for providing generous donations that literally pay for hundreds of people to get back on track, especially through your funding for the Hammer Tower renovation. You are angels!

The entire Foundation board at the Dream Center—you are the most generous people on the planet!

All my homeys in rehab on your way to continued twenty-four-hour victories: keep going! All the homeless families at the DC; all the teens going through recovery; kids in The Movement: you are all absolutely awesome!

Every single donor who has believed in this cause—check it out, sixteen years down, and we are not stopping!

And there's more . . .
GEORGE is grateful to:

Matthew Barnett, for your willingness to work with me, for your patience with the laborious process, your generosity of spirit, and for being the real deal. I learned a lot from you during this journey about leadership, ministry, relationships, trust, and faith. God has used you and your people to further my own transformation.

My family, for doing your best to avoid the cave while I was sequestered during the intense two weeks of writing. You may be used to this drill after forty-six books and all these years, but that doesn't make it any easier for you. Thanks for your patience, sacrifice, prayers, and continual love.

My publishing family at Tyndale, for seeing the importance of this book and moving quickly to get things rolling, and for your help in pulling everything together. Jan Long Harris, thanks for your flights to join us at the Dream Center and then to San Diego to meet with Matthew and me while we were laying the tracks. Doug Knox, thanks for carving time out of your schedule even though it was inconvenient and for flying to the Dream Center to be sure this outrageous story is for real. It is amazing, eh? Thanks for believing in this one. And to all the rest of the team—dozens of people who never get much credit, but who do so much of the work behind the scenes—thank you for your partnership in this project.

Esther Fedorkevich, my agent and great friend, this would still be an idea I talk about at every meeting if you hadn't pushed it into reality. Thanks for your continual support and encouragement and for making things happen. Now you can unpack the boxes in Austin . . .

My good friends who prayed for me throughout this project, read portions of the manuscript and gave feedback, and encouraged me in various ways. This group includes (but is not limited to) Terry Gorka, Steve Russo, Sharon Leavitt, and David Kinnaman, and my colleagues in the Strategenius Group: Connie DeBord, Robert Hawkins, and Joel Tucciarone.

The dozens of people I interviewed, e-mailed, called, and generally bugged for information about the cause within you and how the Dream Center has helped you (and others) optimize it. I am grateful for your openness, honesty, and time.

Marcia Zimmerman and Jan Schuhmacher, who quickly and accurately provided transcripts of the conversations, sharing the insane deadline with me. Your help was invaluable; thanks for rising to the occasion.

Cameron and Mariela Hubiak, who introduced me to the Dream Center, Adopt-A-Block, and all the incredible things that happen at DC-LA. May God bless you two for opening doors and my eyes, and for your faithfulness to Him.

Jesus Christ, who not only saved me but also opened the way for me to pursue the cause within me through the writing of books such as this. Thank You for answering numerous prayers regarding this book. Matthew and I get the author credits, but we pray that You get the glory.

What's the One Great Cause *You* Were Created For?

READING *THE CAUSE WITHIN YOU* could be the start of a new journey in your life. Take the next step and share this book with your friends, family, or church group, and consider what cause you were created for.

Visit www.thecausewithinyou.com for resources to help you continue and share the journey. You will find:

- A printable version of the book discussion guide included in this book
- An expanded, six-session discussion guide designed for use within churches and small groups
- Eight short videos that work with the discussion guides, featuring Pastor Matthew Barnett:
  - An invitation from Pastor Matthew to participate in the book discussion (appropriate for recruiting)
  - Videos to introduce each of the six group discussion sessions
  - Conclusion video
- Six-week sermon series notes for pastors
- Personal evaluation questions and Scriptures to pray and study

- Ideas for causes you can contribute to from the Los Angeles Dream Center
- Links to *The Cause Within You* Facebook forum, where you can share your own stories and experiences and see the stories of others
- Free download of an exclusive song by Dream Center Live, written for *The Cause within You*
- Free downloadable audio file of Pastor Matthew reading Scripture verses related to finding the cause within you

To find out more, visit www.thecausewithinyou.com

Introduction to *The Cause Within You* Discussion Guide

THE CAUSE WITHIN YOU is not a book intended to be simply read; it is a book that should be experienced. While Matthew Barnett's stories are drawn from his work with the Dream Center in Los Angeles, God has placed a cause on each person's heart, and Matthew's goal in writing this book is to help you discover your cause and act upon it wherever you are. To that end, this discussion guide will help you individually or with a group to reflect on, wrestle with, and comprehend the ideas that Matthew presents throughout the book. It will also ask you to draw on your personal experiences to evaluate what you've read and to develop a deeper relationship with God as you pursue the cause within you.

For information about the book and more group discussion resources, visit www.thecausewithinyou.com.

Discussion Guide

CHAPTER 1: A Night on the Streets

1. Matthew says, "I felt uneasy in my gut. That's often how God grabs my attention" (p. 4). Why might God use uneasiness to grab our attention? How does God get your attention? How do you respond?

2. Why does Matthew spend a night on skid row? What insights does he gain from his experience? How do you "demonstrate solidarity with those [you] serve" (p. 5)?

3. Think about a time when God called you to do something outside your comfort zone. What was that experience like? How did you feel? What did God teach you through that experience?

CHAPTER 2: Lost and Found in LA

1. How did Matthew's failure at Bethel Temple open him to the voice of God? How has God spoken to you in your failures?

2. Think about Matthew's "new eyes" (p. 14) to see Echo Park around him. How did his view of the people in this area and

of his reason for being in Los Angeles change? Have you ever experienced a similar eye-opener? Explain.

3. "Sometimes . . . you need to get radical to get right, to get back in touch with the very heartbeat of the cause that lies within you" (p. 16). Have you found this to be true? Explain using personal examples, if possible.

CHAPTER 3: Sidewalk Celebration

1. Matthew says, "Fear cannot own you when a great cause rules your heart" (p. 19). How is this seen in Matthew's skid row experience? Have you seen examples of this elsewhere, either in your own life or in the lives of others? If so, list them.

2. On page 20, Matthew refers to inconvenience as a gift. Have you viewed inconvenience in this way? Why or why not? How might viewing inconvenience as a gift change your perspective in difficult times?

3. Lawrence insists that Matthew bring a Bible with him to skid row, and the Bible changes the way others perceive and interact with Matthew. Why do you think this is? Why does the Bible he brought open opportunities for him to share his faith?

4. Describe Matthew's experience panhandling. How might you feel in similar circumstances? Does his account affect the way you view those who ask you for money? Why or why not?

CHAPTER 4: The Reason to Get Out of Bed

1. What is the benefit of serving others instead of ourselves? What does putting others first look like?

2. "When you carry His load, it is light, especially in comparison to the burdens you create for yourself" (p. 40). When have

you "carried His load" in the past by operating in the areas of your strengths?

3. What does Matthew mean by "our little acts of love have a ripple effect" (p. 44)? Do you agree? Explain with examples.

4. What is the importance of identifying the cause within you now?

5. What do you think of the goal Matthew gives for life: "Use yourself up, doing good wherever you can, until you've got nothing left to give" (p. 50)? What is your initial reaction to this goal? How might your life change if you were to work toward this goal?

CHAPTER 5: Discovering the Cause of a Lifetime

1. What does it mean to "surrender your will to God" (p. 55)? Do you know people who have done this? What characteristics do they share?

2. "Often your cause is revealed when you are at the lowest point of the valley, not on the pinnacle of the mountain" (p. 59). Do you agree? Why do you think this is? How does Alfred's story support Matthew's point?

3. Caroline says, "I asked God in my prayers why it was happening and felt His response was . . . [to ask me] why *I* was allowing it to happen" (p. 67). How might viewing others' suffering as your own responsibility impact the way you serve them?

4. Matthew suggests being open to invitations to serve, since "that invitation might be the beginning of the adventure that identifies the means to filling the hole in your heart" (p. 70). How open are you to invitations to serve? What might it take for you to be more open to such opportunities?

CHAPTER 6: Let Nothing Stand in Your Way

1. "There are things you have to do to survive . . . but the acts that push you beyond survival and provide you with a greater sense of joy are those that make the world a better place" (p. 75). What are the "things you have to do to survive"? Do you feel like you have time for a "cause" in the midst of all your necessary activities? Explain.

2. What do you think of the idea of God's "progressive revelation" (p. 75)? Can you relate to Matthew's experience of progressive revelation in his work with the Dream Center? Give examples.

3. What does Matthew mean by "miracle space" (pp. 77–78)? What are his examples of miracle space? What additional examples can you think of?

4. Have you ever been criticized for following God's call? How did you respond? How can you turn negative criticism to your advantage?

5. Recall the stories that were told in this chapter—of Barry, Matthew, and Alena. What obstacles did they face to fulfilling their causes? How did they overcome those obstacles?

CHAPTER 7: The Power of a Proper Attitude

1. Matthew says, "If I allow my surroundings to dictate my feelings, before I know it, they'll dictate my outcomes, too" (p. 98). What is your reaction to this statement? Have you found it to be true in your own life? Offer examples.

2. What is the benefit of learning to love the stage you're in? Why does Matthew find it crucial to developing a right attitude for service?

3. Discuss Max's story, on pages 106–108. How does Max come to the point of welcoming the homeless family to stay with him?

4. What is the difference between ambition and mission? Why is mission a better motivating factor?

5. What is the importance of "doing your homework" while engaged in a cause? Why does Matthew suggest devoting yourself to "diligence rather than perfection" (p. 113)?

CHAPTER 8: Get It Done

1. What does Matthew mean by "think big and act small"? What are your thoughts on this principle?

2. Why is urgency in meeting needs key in pursuing your cause? How does urgency many times force us to act before we are "ready"? Is this a good thing? Explain.

3. Think about the Dream Center's response to the need created by Hurricane Katrina. How were they able to act so quickly? Imagine how you would act in their situation, and compare and contrast your reaction with theirs.

4. How does Nikki's story illustrate the necessity of earning the right to be heard? How did Nikki earn that right?

5. How can changing the environment affect the fruitfulness of a ministry? Use Matthew's stories of Jake or Emilio and Karina, or your own stories, as illustrations.

CHAPTER 9: Build Your Team to Change the World

1. Why is "partnership . . . a critical element in the pursuit of your dream" (p. 142)?

2. How is the statement "it is incredible how much can be accomplished when you don't care who gets the credit"

(p. 143) exemplified in Matthew's and his dad's roles at the Dream Center?

3. Aaron compares fulfilling one's cause to an addiction. Does this comparison make sense to you? Have you experienced a cause like this? What other images might you use to illustrate fulfilling your cause?

4. Describe your honest thoughts on prayer. What is its purpose in your life? What rules and limitations (if any) do you impose on it?

CHAPTER 10: The Right Time to Quit

1. Describe a time when you felt like quitting. What led you to that point? What was the outcome?

2. Why do you think Matthew advises those who are discouraged in their cause to "give it one more day" (p. 166)?

3. Have you experienced a breakthrough soon after you felt like quitting? Recall your story. How tempted were you to give up before the breakthrough occurred?

4. Why is it important to have balance in life, to "have a life beyond our cause" (p. 175)? How do you seek rest and balance in stressful times?

5. How can focusing on victories help you persevere in your cause?

CHAPTER 11: The Pleasures of Pursuing Your Cause

1. How does the story Matthew tells about Jim Bakker illustrate the importance of having and pursuing a cause in your life?

2. "Serving people gives you a greater motivation to keep on living" (p. 183). Do you agree? Explain.

3. How is joy related to the cause within you? Why is joy a key indicator of a cause?

4. What are the consequences of not pursuing a cause? What are the rewards for doing so?

5. What has been the strongest argument or example Matthew has given in favor of pursuing your cause? How will you move forward after reading this book?

Endnotes

1. 1 John 4:18, NKJV
2. John 3:16
3. Matthew 11:30
4. Mark 12:30-31
5. Hebrews 2:6-7
6. See, for example, Psalm 34:8.
7. Romans 8:31
8. Matthew 6:33
9. Luke 19:17
10. See 1 Samuel 17.
11. Matthew 5:28
12. Hebrews 13:5, NKJV
13. See Jeremiah 1:5.
14. 1 John 4:18, NKJV
15. Romans 5:3-5

About the Authors

MATTHEW BARNETT assumed the pastorate of Bethel Temple in 1994 at the age of twenty. After a life-changing encounter with God, he helped Bethel Temple transition from a traditional-style church to a servant-driven ministry that grew into what is now known as the Dream Center. Compelled by a vision to impact all of Los Angeles by addressing people's physical, material, and spiritual needs in unique and practical ways, the Dream Center has grown into a phenomenon that now reaches more than thirty thousand people each week through its multiple church services and more than two hundred need-centered ministries.

Barnett is also the senior pastor of the historic Angelus Temple, which combined forces with the Dream Center in 2001 in a historic unification of flagship ministries from two different denominations (Foursquare and Assemblies of God). The Sunday services at Angelus Temple now include more than six thousand people per week.

Pastor Barnett is a popular speaker at churches, conventions, conferences, and camp meetings around the world. He has consulted with leading businessmen, celebrities, and athletes, and his efforts have been publicly praised by presidents and major media. He hosts a weekly television program called *The Church That Never Sleeps*, which airs nationally and internationally. He is the author of a pre-vious book, *The Church That Never Sleeps*, and has won numerous awards, including the Religious Heritage Award.

Matthew met Caroline Olsson while she was serving as a volun-teer at the Dream Center. Married in 1999, they have one daughter (Mia Aimee) and one son (Caden West). They reside in Los Angeles. Visit www.matthewbarnett.com.

GEORGE BARNA was first published as a teenager, and he hasn't stopped writing since. He has served as a sportswriter, a speech-writer for public officials, a copywriter for advertising and direct marketing campaigns, and an acclaimed author. As founder of The Barna Group, the nation's leading market research firm focused on the intersection of faith and culture, George has had more than one hundred research-based articles appear in magazines and journals. He is the author of more than forty-five books, including best sell-ers such as *The Frog in the Kettle*, *The Power of Vision*, *Transforming Children into Spiritual Champions*, and *Revolution*. His books have won a variety of awards and have been translated into more than a dozen languages. His Internet reports and blogs have been read by several million people.

George has served as a teaching pastor at a large church in Southern California; has hosted dozens of programs broadcast on CCN; and has taught at Pepperdine, Biola, Dallas Baptist, and Asuza Pacific Universities. Currently the founder of Metaformation, and also a senior partner in the Strategenius Group, he lives with his wife and three daughters in Ventura, California. Visit www.georgebarna.com.

THE CAUSE WITHIN YOU

*Finding the One Great Thing
You Were Created to Do
in This World*

Now available on five unabridged audio CDs
(978-1-4143-4851-3)